"'The world breaks everyone, and afterward, some are strong at the broken places,' Ernest Hemingway wrote. In *The Body Awareness Workbook for Trauma*, Julie Brown Yau provides practical advice based in solid science on how the broken places can become stronger, and how they can heal. This book should be read widely—for who hasn't experienced psychological or physical trauma in our tumultuous world?"

—**Larry Dossey, MD**, author of *One Mind*

"As a clinical psychologist and teacher for those experiencing trauma, I understand how trauma can disconnect us from ourselves, others, and the world around us. I'm therefore truly grateful for Julie Yau's new offering, *The Body Awareness Workbook for Trauma*, in which she provides us with skillful exercises and tools for being able to meet, greet, proactively respond, repair, and heal through trauma. Julie's workbook is valuable and powerful for enabling us to both heal through trauma, and feel connected within ourselves wherever we are, whomever we're with, with whatever circumstances are arising in our body, mind, world, and relationships."

—**Richard Miller, PhD**, founder and chairman of the iRest Institute, and author of *The iRest Program for Healing PTSD*

"This is an unusually intelligent and intricately helpful book. Unusually intelligent in the evidence it gives of its author's familiarity with the complex territory of trauma and its effects on our lives, as well as her ability to write about it with grace and skill. It is intricately helpful because the author gives so many highly refined methods for helping oneself navigate the ravages trauma wreaks on our lives and relationships. *The Body Awareness Workbook for Trauma* is an inspiring blend of grounded theory and effective practice."

—**Don Hanlon Johnson, PhD**, professor in the department of somatics at the School of Professional Psychology and Health at the California Institute of Integral Studies in San Francisco, CA

"*The Body Awareness Workbook for Trauma* is an incredible resource for anyone working through trauma, especially childhood trauma. Julie Brown Yau expertly: 1) Creates a frame of safety, compassion, and hope. 2) Identifies virtually every important component of trauma recovery, which allows people to successfully take small yet meaningful steps toward positive change. 3) Integrates a unique blend of practices from mind-body and spirit to directly help people to improve their lives. While this workbook is written for the general public, every therapist who works with trauma should read it. I highly recommend it."

> —**Robert Schwarz, PsyD, DCEP**, author of *Tools for Transforming Trauma*, and executive director of the Association for Comprehensive Energy Psychology

"I don't see any way through the labyrinth of life without incurring developmental and/or shock trauma. Julie Brown Yau's new book is a powerful and effective way to uncover, heal, and transform through the conscious engagement with your personal trauma. This is an extraordinary fusion of science and spirituality, a work with tremendous value for anyone wishing to become free and live life to the fullest."

> —**Ron Hoffman**, founder and executive director of Compassionate Care ALS, and author of the memoir, *Sacred Bullet*

"In recent years, more of us are discovering the centrality of presence in establishing a balanced and meaningful life. But what is not always understood is how much the existence of traumatic issues in our history can thwart or shut down our ability to stay present. Julie Brown Yau has been exploring this topic for many years, looking at what has been most helpful for people, and seeing how different kinds of trauma respond better to different approaches and therapies. Julie provides a compassionate and practical overview of the diverse forms of trauma, and findings on the most effective methods for working through them. I predict this book will become a classic—both for lay readers seeking help in working through their own difficulties, and for professionals seeking a more complete understanding of this emerging field. Highly recommended."

> —**Russ Hudson**, coauthor of *The Wisdom of the Enneagram* and *Personality Types*

"*The Body Awareness Workbook for Trauma* focuses on the essential missing piece: Spirituality. Trauma is an existential crisis as much as it is psychophysical. The spiritual component is the fulcrum of healing that synthesizes the coherency of self and existence. With this focus, stable, long-lasting healing and transformation is possible."

—**Uma-parvathinatha Saraswati**, spiritual lineage holder Shri Vidya, an ancient integrated system of consciousness development based on Vedic science

"In this comprehensive and deeply insightful guide, Julie has synthesized her vast knowledge and experience in working with trauma with a profound sense of grace and compassion. This is not a dry, theoretical book about trauma, but rather an essential companion for an inner inquiry into all the aspects in which trauma might be coloring the experience of ourselves, others, and the world. This is a step-by-step guide for reclaiming our inherent aliveness and feeling at home in our bodies while authentically expressing our essential self."

—**Zaya Benazzo**, cofounder of Science and Nonduality

THE
BODY AWARENESS
WORKBOOK
FOR TRAUMA

RELEASE TRAUMA FROM YOUR BODY,
FIND EMOTIONAL BALANCE, AND
CONNECT WITH YOUR INNER WISDOM

JULIE BROWN YAU, PhD

REVEAL PRESS
AN IMPRINT OF NEW HARBINGER PUBLICATIONS

Publisher's Note

This publication is designed to provide accurate and authoritative information in regard to the subject matter covered. It is sold with the understanding that the publisher is not engaged in rendering psychological, financial, legal, or other professional services. If expert assistance or counseling is needed, the services of a competent professional should be sought.

NEW HARBINGER PUBLICATIONS is a registered trademark of New Harbinger Publications, Inc.

Distributed in Canada by Raincoast Books

Cover design by Amy Shoup

Interior design by Michele Waters-Kermes and Tracy Carlson

Acquired by Elizabeth Hollis Hansen

Edited by Kristi Hein

Library of Congress Cataloging-in-Publication Data on file

Printed in the United States of America

24   23   22

10 9 8 7 6 5

Contents

Foreword

I know Dr. Julie Brown Yau through the beautiful work she does for Compassionate Care ALS. She developed the Cultivating Compassion Education Series and offers counseling support for people affected by ALS and other traumatic diseases. Her thirty-year skill set in psychological, somatic, and spiritual practices blends in a unique and wonderful way to aid others to resolve trauma, reduce suffering, and find joy.

As a writer who has spent a good deal of time over the past fifteen years with people living with fatal neurodegenerative diseases, I'm familiar with the trauma sustained by these kinds of diagnoses and journeys. Alzheimer's, Huntington's, and ALS have no disease-modifying treatments. There are no cures. There are no survivors.

In addition to the physical burdens of these diseases, there are the psychological, emotional, and spiritual ones. People with diseases of the brain are often excluded from community, feared by those who fear their illnesses. The diagnosed become *other-ized*—isolated, alienated, stigmatized, shamed, disconnected. Whether due to the limitations imposed on them by their disease or the rejection by others who fear and ignore them, people diagnosed with these neurodegenerative diseases lose their jobs, freedoms, friends, passions, identities, independence, dreams, and ultimately, their lives.

And yet, without donning rose-colored glasses, I also see what can be gained. Sometimes, remarkably, people find hope in the most hopeless of situations. They let go of grudges. They forgive and ask for forgiveness. They rewire their thinking, focusing their minds only on what matters now—loving the people they love, helping others while they still can, no longer sweating the small stuff, enjoying one more Christmas, one more sunny day at the beach. A friend of mine, devastated in a million ways by an unexpected diagnosis of young-onset Alzheimer's, once said to me, "There are gifts that come with this disease, if you choose to open them."

How do some people do this? How do they move from feeling victimized and shattered to feeling gratitude and wholeness? How do some people have the capacity to transform during and following such catastrophic traumas—to find inner peace and joy even as life is being stripped away?

Many times, I have witnessed the kind of healing Julie shepherds. Whether it's the trauma of a fatal diagnosis and the losses that accompany it, abuse, divorce, a broken heart, feeling unloved, post-traumatic stress, or developmental trauma, Julie offers us insights, skills, and practices to reduce suffering and find healing. Through exercises that focus on breathing, gratitude, and compassion, a new awareness can be cultivated. Negative thoughts, limiting beliefs, and reactive behaviors that don't serve us can be released, reestablishing a sense of safety and well-being in mind, body, and spirit, even in the midst of something as unsafe as ALS or Alzheimer's. Our brains are not forever hardwired, stuck in a traumatic way of thinking, feeling, believing, and behaving. Through the techniques and tools that Julie offers in this book, we can form new connections and activate new pathways that lead to safer thoughts, feelings, and behaviors.

At the root of most suffering is the experience of being disconnected. In *The Body Awareness Workbook for Trauma*, Julie guides us back to a deep connection within ourselves. She shows us how to shed the barriers that we may have built to protect ourselves from trauma—barriers with which we have also unwittingly disconnected us from others, our own feelings, and our own hearts—to reveal our authentic selves, ready for reconnection, expression, freedom, and growth.

—Lisa Genova, PhD

The Journey to Post-Traumatic Growth

If you've purchased this book, you're most likely living with the consequences of some form of trauma. Humans are naturally hardwired to recover from trauma. Yet sometimes traumatic events are so overwhelming, and the necessary support so hard to find, that recovery doesn't happen. Trauma *is* a normal part of life; continued suffering from its effects need not be.

This book is designed to help you resolve trauma by exploring, reflecting on, and participating in the exercises each day that you're able.

My goal is to empower you with skills, practices, and insights that will help you heal from the ongoing repercussions of trauma and adversity within your whole body system. Rather than presenting complex technical descriptions of the neurological processes involved in trauma responses, I offer a basic, comprehensive scientific, psychobiological, and spiritual perspectives of trauma and its symptoms, and exercises to help you recover from your experience of trauma while developing resilience—the ability to bounce back from challenging or traumatic incidents. The exercises are designed to help you recover from your body's unresolved response to traumas. I provide clear explanations of why and how these exercises will assist you on your healing journey, and how the associated spiritual potential can revitalize your life.

Because the trauma experience is embedded in your body—that is, it touches all your body systems—it must be addressed through your body and body awareness. The body includes your brain and nervous system and thus related to your thought processes, emotions, perceptions, imagination, and rational thinking.

Your safety is paramount. As much as you need to be in touch with your embedded trauma, it is vital that you connect with what was not available to you at the time of the trauma. Achieving this, through the exercises and skills provided, can shift both your physiology and your psychology, diminishing or dissolving the consequences of trauma.

TRAUMA AND SPIRITUALITY

Trauma and spirituality may seem to be radically different, yet these aspects of your experience are intimately and inextricably connected. To simplify and clarify spirituality in the context of trauma work, I describe the relationship between trauma and spirituality as occurring along a continuum. Trauma work inevitably opens you up to spirituality.

Let's define spirituality, for now, as a deepening connection first to your innermost being and then to others. This means authentically expressing your unique self in relationship with others and the world. Deepening your sense of spirituality is very much like the process involved in resolving trauma. As you heal, and the web of survival strategies or defenses from trauma diminishes, you restore your connection to and expression of your essential self. This opens you to a deeper spiritual reality and/or perspective of self, others, the world, and, if you like, the cosmos.

POST-TRAUMATIC GROWTH

You may have been waiting for years to transform the constrictions and fears that have haunted you. You may have just come to understand how the complications of trauma are limiting your life. Now the possibilities of healing beckon. You *can* heal from acute or shock traumas that occurred at any time in your life. You can overcome early developmental trauma, to gain a flexible inner strength and greater resilience, and become a more compassionate human being. You can free all expressions of your authentic being from the repression, disconnection, or dissociation that has restricted your experience of full aliveness and joy and blocked your inherent wisdom. The underlying principle of all relationship is love. And when there is love, healing happens. When healing happens, you'll know love *and* wisdom, and you'll act from these essential qualities of being.

Based on extensive brain and body research into trauma responses and ways to heal, post-traumatic growth (PTG) enables managing life's challenges to emerge healthier, feeling a greater sense of agency—a sense of being competent and self-reliant—and a deeper appreciation of life itself. You can embrace every facet of your humanness, your relationships can become deeper and more meaningful, and your spirituality may expand and strengthen.[1]

Circumstances, events, or trauma symptoms that may feel crushing to you now may bring unexpected gifts of human spirit, of creativity, confidence, and a new life narrative. You can develop a healthy relationship with emotions that may now feel overwhelming and frightening, such as shame, sadness, anger, and rage. As you integrate the experiences of the unresolved traumatic past, you broaden your emotional communication and your own emotional and spiritual intelligence.

As you go through the workbook, you may experience a profound sense of meaning and expansion in your life, developing and enjoying your new life narrative, a story of triumph and success.

BODY AWARENESS AS A GATEWAY TO HEALING TRAUMA

With trauma attracting greater attention in the fields of psychology, affective and contemplative neuroscience, and spirituality, I can draw on a wide and rich array of integrative interdisciplinary theories. As trauma's serious impact is more widely acknowledged, the silence surrounding this terrible problem is being broken. More people are realizing the effects of trauma in their lives and finding their way through the rigors of trauma's consequences to joyous well-being.

Humans can change themselves for the better. This book's exercises can enliven your whole body with life force and creativity, invigorate or calm you, and bring you into the present, rather than living with your lingering unresolved past or in disconnection or collapse. You'll cultivate a greater sense of the natural presence of the divine, which many spiritual traditions and religions believe is always present. There is no other place to go but *here*, with all your vitality and capacity to *be*, cultivating your capacity for deep presence and awareness. However, most of us must purposefully work to open to this state of being or to allow its natural grace.

Unresolved, trauma continues to live in your body. Following a traumatic experience, how you feel inside your body, even the way you hold your body, colors your perception of yourself and the world. Your body is either perpetually scared, on high alert and overly vigilant, or shut down and disconnected to varying degrees. This creates an inner tension that heightens your perception of actual and potential danger, consciously and/or unconsciously. Fear blocks your inherent love and wisdom. Your body may not know that the trauma and danger is long past, even though you're rationally aware of this.

It's important to feel balanced and grounded in this world. As you work toward realizing your dreams and nourishing your spirituality, I'm standing by you, both metaphorically and energetically, through this workbook's pages and in the online recording of some exercises (which you can find at http://www.newharbinger.com/43256).

As you learn and practice the exercises, you'll find an intimacy and connection with your body that you may not have known before. You'll learn to freely express yourself with a clear, strong voice with robust boundaries, to live to the personal rhythm of your heart's deepest desire.

YOUR MOST SACRED RELATIONSHIP

Your most important relationship is with *yourself*. In the context of this book, this means living as an integrated and interconnected self, a spontaneous and embodied being—grounded, vibrant, at home in your body, authentically expressing your essential self.

When trauma disrupts or obscures your relationship with your inherent being, all other relationships are compromised. Without a healthy relationship with yourself, you're vulnerable to depression, shame, anxiety, headaches, lack of self-worth, lack of a sense of safety, self-judgment, intrusive thoughts, and loss of connection with others. And many physical ailments have been traced to trauma.

You might not know that your naturally loving relationship to yourself has been interrupted in some manner, although to some of you it may be obvious. No one would purposely break this sacred relationship, yet it can happen when you experience trauma.

Trauma, at its core, creates disconnection—an inability to be fully present with your own being and with others. After trauma you may suffer from many emotionally, mentally, and physically painful feelings that cause you to isolate, withdraw, or compromise yourself in other ways. Trauma creates fear, either conscious or unconscious. Fear separates you from love—the love that you are, and the love you could share with others. All this disconnection can be terribly painful. You may feel acutely alone, misunderstood, not seen or heard, at odds with others. You may lack self-esteem or feel overly prideful, which creates further separation. You may feel you're a horrible person, or that the world is a cold and empty place. Or you may be sure you can work out everything rationally. You may be self-critical, feel disconnected spiritually, or be excessively judgmental. Hidden rage may escape in angry outbursts. We'll address these symptoms of unresolved trauma throughout this workbook, as you reconnect to your being.

YOUR PHYSICAL (BIOLOGICAL) AND SUBTLE (ENERGETIC) BODIES

I was fifteen when the practice of meditation came into my life, bringing with it silent gifts and a guiding hand. My father was an aikido teacher and 5th dan master, and through that practice

I directly experienced a sense of spirituality, the importance of inhabiting the physical body, and the sense of a *subtle body*—an energetic body that surrounds and permeates the physical. I remember the quiet meditation of our sitting before practice, and how easily this resonated with me. I experienced my own being—a quiet, spacious presence and aliveness—and interconnectedness with others, the world and beyond.

In both aikido and meditation, by tuning in to my body sensations, I could feel what in traditional martial arts is called *life energy*. I also call it *life force*. Life force is believed to be a principle element of anything living; it is part of the *subtle energies* of Eastern philosophy, the *prana* of Indian cultures, *pneuma* of ancient Greece, and *vital force* of Western philosophy. The intricacies and maps of the subtle energies, body and physiology, vary from tradition to tradition, yet they share a view of this invisible subtle body—which includes channels, points, and chakras—in which the flow of subtle life force energy (think of acupuncture) determines the characteristics and well-being of the visible physical body. You'll work with these principles in some of the exercises here.

In aikido we refer to this life force as *ki* (you may know it as "chi"). It's the basis of all matter, every phenomenon, emotion, sense, will, consciousness, and conscience. It's part of the makeup of the breath, just as prana is in the yogic traditions. Ki connects our body, our mind, and the cosmos. However, when you have unresolved trauma it's rather difficult to maintain intimate awareness of life force and its relationship to these connections.

After trauma, ki is distorted, repressed, or disconnected. This creates rigidity and feelings of being stuck in the body or mind. Healing trauma that embraces body awareness reweaves that life force back into you, returning you to a state of harmony and connection. For instance, when emotions are too overwhelming, you may automatically repress or dissociate them. These emotions—your life energy—still affect you, even though you don't feel them. You're also using your life force to suppress the emotions below your conscious awareness. It's exhausting, but most of us do it unconsciously. Rather than flowing freely through you, being part of your creative expression and feelings of aliveness, that energy remains stagnant, creating body tension and mental agitation. With this book, you'll learn techniques for releasing stagnant energy and emotions through the body, so you may connect more deeply to your experience and live with more vitality. You may restore your natural life force flow and realize its distinct relationship to spirituality and a deeper, intuitive way of knowing.

Your life force fuels self-expression, intuition, healthy aggression, sexuality, passions, creativity, and heart's desire. It allows you to feel alive and joyous. It's also the energy that allows you to fight or flee to safety in a traumatic event. During trauma you get a natural surge of this life force. Afterward, if you don't use, discharge, or integrate it, it negatively affects your physiology and psychology, diminishing your aliveness and vibrancy.

There is one positive effect of not immediately releasing traumatic energy after a traumatic event: the potential to use this energy for PTG and expanding your consciousness in your healing process.

Your body's inherent wisdom will naturally move you toward healing—toward connection, aliveness, and your deepest longing, previously obscured by trauma.

HOW TO USE THIS WORKBOOK

Many books about trauma are, understandably, directed primarily at psychotherapists. Therapy is often key to healing trauma, and it's crucial for therapists to know and understand new and promising information, to provide the best possible treatment. The relational model of therapist and patient can be a rich, reparative, and integrative experience of healing, growth, and development. However, not everyone who wants to heal from trauma has the resources or desire to enter therapy.

This book is not a substitute for therapy; indeed, it can be a great support to use while in therapy. But it is a stand-alone book that can help you reconnect to your body and body awareness, integrate disconnected parts of yourself, and restore your nervous system to harmony and coherence. It's a guide to exploring your inner world as you connect to the world around you.

The healing process is not linear; it's a winding, up-and-down road. Yet over time you'll feel an increased sense of aliveness, renewed space for joy, and enhanced capacity for *presence*. Your interpersonal relationships will improve. And, most important, as your inherent wisdom emerges, your naturally loving relationship to your innermost being will be restored.

You can use the book chronologically. Go through each chapter slowly, practicing the exercises to build your foundation of safety (paramount in the trauma healing process) and learn how to ground, orient, and resource yourself. This gradually develops a deep capacity for body awareness (often called *somatic awareness*) while enhancing your capacity for self and emotional regulation. Your imagination is a powerful tool for transformation and for renewing your relationship with your body. I introduce it initially because your imagination specifically supports your capacity for body awareness; through it you can begin to be present with vital elements that were not there to support you when trauma happened.

You can browse through the chapters to find exercises and practices that feel useful for you; learn about trauma healing so you know you're not skipping steps; and find what will inspire, motivate, or calm you. You may want to begin by cultivating compassion. At times you may need to invigorate your body with life force, using the subtle body practices, then return to earlier exercises to finish addressing thwarted defense mechanisms. Be gentle in reconnecting with your body, especially if you have early childhood trauma. Take your time and allow each step to be truly integrating, bringing you closer to unity and wholeness.

You can engage the book as a companion and carry it with you to know you're not alone as you walk this path. As deepening bodily experiences happen, note them in your workbook or a journal, recording what you learn and feel in new ways.

You can experience the book with your therapist, or a companion, to enhance your journey of connection and healing and to work in greater depth. You can experience deeper, more bountiful healing when supported and witnessed by another. And as trauma is also relational, I encourage you to seek companionship in general. Beyond the traumatic events themselves, for many trauma victims either the absence of another person or the presence of a threatening other allowed those events to become embedded in the body. Having the loving or supportive eyes and presence of another when we are scared allows our whole system to calm and settle.

However you use the book, may it help you imagine the life potential awaiting you on this journey. May you find healing with ease and grace.

CHAPTER 1

Gently Explore Your Trauma Experience

You're embarking on a courageous journey and exploration of your innermost being. I'm excited and honored to be your guide. I know how terrible trauma can be, and I know how exhilarating and empowering it can feel to be healed from trauma's devastating effects. As you begin this healing journey, know that it can be a positive and life-affirming experience.

Trauma may be affecting you physiologically, emotionally, psychologically, spiritually, and socially. It may be outwardly obvious to you and others, or you may be suffering inwardly, silently, and even confused about your pain and its origin even as you're drawn to explore the work of healing trauma. You may be suffering with the consequences of a traumatic impact from an accident, a devastating divorce, abuse, war, or a natural disaster. You may realize you're dealing with the result of not having your essential needs met as a child (needs for love, attunement, holding, nurturing, mirroring, nourishment, acknowledgment), unavoidable extended separation from your primary caregiver, or severe neglect—these are part of developmental trauma, from what *didn't* happen for you, what you *didn't* receive. Lack of nurturance disrupts the development of brain processes that help us develop a unified sense of self and resilience.[2] This can create many layers of disconnection and even feel life-threatening.

Although the symptoms of developmental trauma and of shock or acute trauma often look the same, they need to be addressed differently. As you explore your interior world through the exercises here, you'll begin to recognize what applies to you through recognition, insight, practice, and the ensuing transformation.

Once you begin the resolution process, you'll start to emerge from trauma's innate constriction and generate a positive, lasting expansion of your consciousness. Transforming trauma—rather than disregarding, burying, or shutting it away—can lead to positive restoration and reemergence of your unique self and full vitality. You can uncover remarkable, hitherto unrecognized aspects of your being—strengths, creative potential, wisdom, and compassion.

I don't mean to romanticize trauma in any way. You know how it can rob you of the fullness of life, connection, intimacy, and joy. You may feel like your previously known, innermost self has died—or that you've never fully known that innermost being. But trauma healing can be regenerative. Experiencing this renewal takes conscious intention, courage, creation of the right conditions, and support. Generating self-compassion, loving kindness, and other positive qualities will be a key to finding union with your whole being and beyond.

This workbook is part of your new support system. Let's begin with your focusing on what *you* would like to receive from using this workbook and healing trauma as a whole. If it's too difficult to imagine yourself on the other side of trauma right now, imagine a person who has traits that you would love to generate within yourself. As this becomes easier to imagine, come back to this exercise.

EXERCISE: Myself, Healed

Spend a few moments imagining and feeling a positive and lasting transformation that you would like to have happen on this healing journey. Use your senses to imagine, feel, hear, taste, and even smell your transformed self. For example, once you heal from trauma, what will you feel like inside that differs from today? Confident, connected, open, joyful, alive, trusting, fearless?

_____

_____

How will you hold yourself? Perhaps elegantly upright, soft and open, joyfully expressive?

_____

_____

What will your relationship with your body be like? Respectful, reverent, generous?

_____

_____

How will you be in relationship to yourself and others? Loving, honoring, intimately honest?

_____

_____

As you imagined, did you notice any changes in your body sensations, emotions, or thoughts? Did you feel hopeful or excited? Do you have clarity yet about what you would like to happen as you heal, live your life, and bring your dreams to life? If not, note any positive experiences you did notice in the exercise.

_____

_____

_____

You're realizing that through healing of your trauma you can create a future connected to your most authentic and essential self. This workbook will help you to:

- Reconnect to your body, emotions, and vital aliveness

- Reconnect to your capacity for self- and emotional regulation

- Bolster your experience of safety

- Develop resilience to further trauma

- Create a sense of self-sufficiency and an internal locus of control

- Resolve underlying negative beliefs and strengthen self-esteem

- Resolve self-sabotaging inner conflicts and dissolve defenses

- Complete thwarted biological responses

- Heal the wounds of your early parental relationships

- Reconnect to creative pursuits and spiritual and cultural expression

As you embark on this path of healing multiple trauma elements (most people have a combination), you'll no longer be on an encoded course set by trauma. You'll be releasing the bonds that keep you emotionally enslaved to your trauma survival responses.

Your conscious intentions and mental efforts play an essential role in determining your evolving physical world.[3] You can express an intention as a short statement made as if it is already happening (these statements are also called *affirmations*). Setting an intention is a wonderful way for your thoughts and life force energy to begin to move toward your desired healing outcome. For example: *I am easily and gracefully connecting with my body and emotions, while feeling a deep sense of intimacy with my partner. Or I am feeling vitality and a creative force that allows me to fulfill my potential as a…* Try it here:

- I am _____

- I am _____

- I am _____

As you consider your intentions, you may see what you want for yourself and your life. As your body awareness and observation skills deepen and you create a more intimate relationship with your body, you'll also see what you do that *gets in the way* of your getting what you want. The impact of trauma creates internal dilemmas that sabotage or disrupt those wants, mostly unconsciously. Internal conflicts are exhausting and keep you *stuck* in a trauma response. You'll be creating interruptions in those survival patterns, making new positive and creative possibilities available. There is a strong positive correlation between your conscious intentions and your bodily actions.[4] This can revitalize the meaning of your unfolding life story as you recognize the remarkable role your mind plays, in relationship with your body, in determining your future. As you gain clarity on your heart's desire and your trauma-free life, you can create new and improved, more specific intentions.

YOUR UNIQUE EXPERIENCE OF TRAUMA

The consequences of trauma vary greatly and are unique for each person. These may include great destruction and despair, feelings of insurmountable grief, a myriad of physical symptoms, sometimes serious psychopathology, and, on the more positive side, post-traumatic growth (PTG) as the person develops and expands through consciously engaging with the adversities faced. It's important not to diminish or dismiss the devastating effects of trauma—especially repetitive, ongoing trauma—by simply calling trauma an opportunity for personal growth. However, as noted in the introduction, research demonstrates trauma's potential for both psychological and spiritual growth and development. Also, looking for the hopeful or positive allows your body to move toward that.

Your unique experience of trauma emerges from your personal history, genetic resiliency, spiritual perspective, the length and severity of the traumatic event/s, and your emotional and psychobiological states in the moment of the initial traumatic impact(s) and the moments following. Who was there or not there and how they respond are also crucial determinants of whether you become traumatized by potentially traumatic events and threatening experiences.

The more you learn about your unique experience of trauma, the less problematic it will become to address it and heal from its effects. And although healing trauma is not a linear process, over time you'll experience changes at every level of your being.

THE VARIED SYMPTOMS OF TRAUMA

People who live with unresolved trauma experience it in different ways. Some have a wide variety of symptoms, such as depression, anxiety, intrusive thoughts, gastrointestinal issues, emotional instability, insomnia, and inability to attend to or even know their own needs; others report only a few. Some people remain unaware that they suffer from any consequences of trauma; others don't recognize that there were incidents or times in their lives that were traumatizing, yet they experience symptoms typical of trauma's consequences. Such symptoms— panic, mental intrusions, unresolved grief, isolation, lack of self-worth, shame—may not show up until weeks, months, or even years after the initial traumatic event. When they do, it can be difficult to connect them to the trauma. This is especially true for trauma that emerged in your early years—even more so when trauma arose from not having your essential needs met. But this is also true of shock trauma.

RECONNECTION AFTER TRAUMA

Trauma creates various degrees of disconnection—from your body, emotions, core self, others, and the world around you. Disconnection feels so terribly painful that you adapt strategies to hide this pain even from yourself. We humans are hardwired for connection, so healing trauma is about connecting or reconnecting to your core self (some call this their *authentic being* or *essential nature*); with this deep connection you can know and express your emotions, needs, desires—all of who you truly are. You'll find a deep sense of inner freedom. Although this may sound quite abstract, you'll move toward direct experience of this by uncovering and resolving the layers of traumas consequences.

This inner freedom opens you to your heart's deepest longing or desire. You may have given this up in childhood during adverse or traumatic times, to survive the threat you felt, or closed yourself off to it in acute or shock traumas. Developmental or acute trauma always brings a sense of threat, pushing you to limit yourself for protection or survival. In the healing process of reconnection, as those limitations begin to diminish, you'll begin to feel how you fit into the order of things, experiencing a renewed sense of presence and ease.

As the gravitational field of your heart's desire envelops you, your life can simply flow, in harmony with the rhythm of something greater than yourself. In this sense healing trauma is intimately connected to spirituality.

INTEGRATION IS KEY IN YOUR HEALING

Integration helps you link together elements of your experiences that may have become disconnected through traumatic experiences.[5] Over time, integration of the split-off or repressed parts of your experience (such as difficult emotions, fear, parts of your young consciousness) restores your ability to function at your best and feel safe, grounded, and fully alive. You'll explore more of this key to healing in later chapters.

THE OUTCOME OF HEALING

Rather than focusing on the many symptoms and consequences of trauma now, you're going to look ahead at the positive experiences possible in healing and resolution—to deepen your initial intention by envisioning more specific ways you'd like to feel and be when you've healed. The following exercise lists potential changes, to bring you positive focus and incentive for your life beyond trauma.

EXERCISE: How I Envision Myself Healed

In the Now column, check the changes you would like to accomplish; this allows energy to flow toward what you would like to have happen that you're aware of now, without dwelling on their present absence, or how to get there. As you pursue your healing work, check the Over Time column when this item becomes a reality for you. And as your healing evolves, keep coming back to this list to note what is transforming.

Physical	Now	Over Time
Feeling grounded in my body		
A sense of expansion, spaciousness, lightness, aliveness in my body		
Ability to set limits and boundaries, to say no		
Acceptance of and tending to my personal needs		
Ease in touching and being touched and in choosing in what ways		
Ability and desire to be intimate with my partner		
A deep capacity for physical sensations		
A sense of uprightness and strength with flexibility		
Emotional	**Now**	**Over Time**
A feeling of empowerment		
A feeling of connection with self, others, and the world around me		
A feeling of calm even in times of uncertainty		
Capacity to regulate emotions		
Capacity to laugh and not take myself too seriously		
A vital feeling of openness, aliveness, and joyful anticipation of life		
Ability to experience a wide range of emotions without feeling overwhelmed		
Capacity to feel anger and aggression without acting it out toward others or inward toward myself		

Cognitive	Now	Over Time
Capacity to concentrate and focus		
Ability to appreciate multiple perspectives		
Positive thinking about myself and life		
Natural curiosity about even challenging things		
Capacity for insights		
Creative perception and expression		
Enjoyment of diverse opinions and capacity to hold multiple perspectives		
Acceptance of what I once rejected about myself		
Behavioral	**Now**	**Over Time**
Ability to maintain strong yet flexible boundaries		
Ability to know and meet my essential needs		
Ability to use a range of resources		
Ability to self-soothe when stressed		
Ability to stay connected with myself when I connect with others		
Social	**Now**	**Over Time**
Ability to feel comfortable in a variety of social situations		
Comfort with participating in a variety of activities that I previously felt I could not		
Ability to stay present when engaging with others		
Desire for the company of others		
Healthy balance between work and play		
Healthy balance between "me time" and time with others		

Spiritual	Now	Over Time
Trust in the unfolding of life events		
Deep awareness of being connected to something beyond myself		
Feelings of gratitude, compassion, and loving kindness for myself and others		
Feeing of expansion and lightness in my body		
Ability to focus on goodness, even when the situation feels bad		

How was this exercise for you? Did you feel any sense of hope, excitement, or possibility that you had previously been unaware of? Revisit this exercise frequently to see if there are new outcomes you would like to move toward, as you realize ways in which you're not as connected as you would like to be.

WHEN YOU PERCEIVE A THREAT

When a frightening or traumatic event happens, your body/mind perceives a threat. Your primitive brain—the part that's responsible for survival responses—prepares you for fight, flight, freeze, or immobility. It instinctively inventories the current elements: sounds, smells, temperature, people, colors, time of year. After the initial trauma, in the future those elements can become unrecognized cues of danger. When one or more of these elements is present, that primitive part of your brain that perceives danger or threat becomes aroused and alert.

Past experiences can affect you in the present even without distinct, conscious memories or connection to the original traumatic event. Because the very sensate specifics of your senses of the initial memory are often unconscious, you may find yourself reacting negatively in situations without knowing why. This can be quite confusing. Without even having to know or remember every trauma that happened, by cultivating body awareness and presence, you'll facilitate a psychobiological shift that will begin to heal the trauma.

Your body, with all its intricate systems, is remarkable. When you bring your awareness to your body, healing your relationship with it, this naturally allows harmony and coherence among all systems. Your body will allow its innate capacity for wisdom to come to fruition, which is self-healing. You're creating the conditions for this as you make your way through the exercises and practices here. You're giving yourself a wonderful gift, and even though you'll not always feel good—because healing trauma is not linear and often feels tumultuous—the outcome can be joyous, satisfying, and incredibly nourishing.

WAYS TO GROUND AND SELF-SOOTHE DURING TRAUMA HEALING WORK

Because simply reading about trauma may activate your ingrained responses, here's a technique you can use any time you feel your body tensing, numb, or becoming more uncomfortable.

EXERCISE: Grounding and Orienting

This simple yet powerful grounding and calming tool will become part of your self-soothing toolbox. (An audio recording of instructions for this exercise is available at http://www.newharbinger.com/43256.) Practice the exercise now, even if you're feeling fine, to become familiar with it. Return to it any time you need to as you make your way through the workbook and in your day-to-day life.

1. Sit in a comfortable, supportive chair. Notice the state of your body. Are you relaxed, tense, nervous, calm? Your body may feel numb, fearful, tingling, trembling, or agitated. You may notice feeling disoriented or becoming emotional or disconnected. Record what you're experiencing. Simply describing what you notice may begin the calming process.

    _____

    _____

    _____

2. Feel your feet contacting the floor. Slightly press your soles against the floor and feel the sensation.

3. Notice your bottom on the seat of your chair. Sink into the chair and press your back into it, letting it support you.

4. Now look around the room. Move your head and neck slowly as you take in your surroundings. *It's important to move your neck and head as you look around, not just your eyes.* Look in front of you, to both sides, and maybe even behind you. Be aware of your breathing. Notice what happens to your breath; see if it deepens and your body relaxes slightly.

5. If your body takes a spontaneous deep breath, feel the exhale and notice how your body responds to that breath. (It will likely feel good.)

6. Find an image of a person smiling broadly. Look into the picture and smile back. This will have a calming effect on your nervous system, and your body will begin to feel a sense of safety.

If your reading of this book—your taking this initial step to face your trauma—has shifted you into a state of heightened tension, with this grounding exercise you may notice your body and mind are more relaxed. Relax into any slight softening, release of tension, or less tightness that you may feel. You're gently connecting with your body.

Now record what you experienced as you practiced the exercise. Your experience is any dimension of your being—body, thoughts, emotions, memories, images, perceptions.

_____

_____

_____

How does it feel to record your experience after the exercise? By bringing your awareness to your experience, you may be feeling more, or you may simply be more aware that you're *not* feeling. You're starting to activate your natural healing response, deepening your awareness and cultivating presence and curiosity.

THE IMPACT OF A TRAUMATIC EVENT

An overwhelming event—such as a car accident, a terminal diagnosis, a fall, physical abuse, an emotional blow such as a divorce or a death, or a natural disaster—is often referred to as an *acute* or *shock trauma*. When you experience the impact of an unexpected or very frightening event, the acute trauma shocks you, sending a jolt through your nervous system. You can't grasp the full significance of this type of traumatic event in the moment, so it creates a trauma response in your body. As you likely already know, trauma lives in your body, not in the traumatic events.

Typically, there is also an intense wave of emotion, too intense to digest at the time and in the immediate aftermath. For instance, you might feel intense sadness, anger, or rage at what has just happened. Along with the jolt, these normal yet powerful emotions disrupt your cognitive capacity to sort through what happened and process your experience. All of this creates an internal *disorganization* in which your body is unable to return to a state of balance. These emotions remain but are repressed or *split off* from consciousness, which causes disturbances in your body/mind until they're integrated. There are many more elements of disorganization that occur within your body/mind system in the face of trauma. As you make your way through the workbook, you'll gain more knowledge, understanding, and of course ways to return organization to your body systems.

DEVELOPMENTAL TRAUMA IN INFANCY AND BEYOND

When your essential needs (detailed early in this chapter) are not met when you're young, it can feel dreadful inside your body, then and *now*, as the trauma is embedded throughout your body. Sadly, you probably didn't know it was the environment that was insufficiently responding to you and letting you down. All you know is that you don't feel good inside; you internalize these experiences as *your own failures*. When something bad happens, you feel it's *you* who are bad. You adapt to these early life conditions with a strategy that ultimately limits your authentic self yet allows you to feel you can survive. You can go through your life with an inner sense of "badness" about yourself that really was *not you*. Or your organism may perceive the world as unsafe because of external circumstance, dysregulating your body systems, so your body feels unsafe to inhabit. Or your perception of the world and others remains stuck in survival mode and erroneous beliefs—nothing is safe, no none can be trusted, you lack self-worth, or you need to fight to survive. These are just a few of the erroneous beliefs that can emerge within you as a child, that you internalize and live by, often unconsciously. These erroneous beliefs often sabotage your current life without your consciously recognizing it.

THE DEVELOPMENT OF WHAT YOU IDENTIFY WITH

Developmental trauma can affect your self-esteem and self-worth, leaving you feeling terrible about yourself. You identify at an early age with these distorted thoughts and feelings that strongly link with messages about yourself. Because this sense of inherent "badness" and other false perceptions become encoded within you, your thought processes can't completely override the feelings.

So developmental trauma isn't only about what may have happened to you but also what *didn't* happen for you in your developing years—your essential needs weren't met, you didn't experience safety in your body and emotions, and you couldn't express yourself authentically in the world.

You may have felt anger, shame, or guilt, and/or completely shut down in response to the failure of your caregivers and environment to meet your essential needs. Shutting down is a survival response to threat in which your sensory alertness and orienting to the environment are inhibited. Typically, body motion ceases (immobility) and heart rate slows (bradycardia), with little or no sympathetic nervous system activity.[6] You can see the shutdown response in an infant, child, or adult with a blank face and stare. Their muscle tone may also be flaccid. The impulse to shut down is propelled by terror—it's fear potentiated. This response emerges when an individual perceives fear and inescapability[7] and can occur with both developmental and acute traumas.

The experience of not having your needs met as a child is very frightening and simply too much to bear, so typically you will disconnect from the unbearable feelings and emotions. Sadly, the effects on your body and brain don't just go away. It can mean a lifelong impact of nervous system dysregulation, a mind filled with unrelenting negative beliefs and feelings about yourself and the world, and bodily discomfort. When your caregivers do not attune to or satisfy your needs consistently, there are communication inaccuracies between the right and left hemispheres of your brain. This diminishes the left brain's capacity to process overwhelming emotion, leading to fragmentation of mental processes, emotional dysregulation, and disconnection from the body.[8] If you grew up without reliable closeness to others or shared nonverbal communication, the right hemisphere's functioning seemingly fades, and you may become left hemisphere dominant,[9] a survival strategy that denies you the ability to experience the richness of a socially and intimately engaged life, a secure feeling of safety in the body, and the full range of emotions.

These stressful relational perceptions of your infancy or childhood are encrypted in the unconscious of the right brain, not the left. By accessing your body and imagination through metaphor and visualization (as you'll do throughout this workbook), you'll engage your right brain and replace old encrypted perceptions with healthier new ones. It's a whole-body, whole-brain approach to healing trauma.

Trauma reduces your capacity for self and emotional regulation and integration. Self-regulation allows you to sleep when you need to, to know when you need to rest, to have healthy ways to release stress and return to a state of inner balance. Emotional self-regulation allows you to experience and handle sadness, grief, joy, excitement, fear, anger, and happiness rather than disconnecting from or avoiding them.

The good news is, your brain is pliable throughout your life, and your body has an inherent imperative to heal. As you nurture these capacities, you can become the person you long to be, in a body and in expression that feels joyful and safe.

EXERCISE: How Do You Feel About Yourself?

Reflect on each question and identify how you may now be experiencing the effects of developmental trauma. Circle Yes or No.

- Do you have an inner sense of badness about yourself?   Yes   No

- Are you challenged with feelings of unworthiness?   Yes   No

- Do you often feel unheard or unseen by others?   Yes   No

- Do you sense that there is something fundamentally flawed within you?   Yes   No

- Do you avoid conflict?   Yes   No

- Do you secretly feel helpless?   Yes   No

- Do you often feel scared, yet don't know why?   Yes   No

- Do you fear being rejected or abandoned?   Yes   No

- Do you experience shame?   Yes   No

- Do you feel unsafe in your body and the world?   Yes   No

Are there any other ways you feel about yourself that were not listed?

_____

_____

Take a moment after this exercise and notice how you feel. There may be all kinds of emotions and sensations, or numbness. Simply evaluate what you feel right now. Whatever may not feel good right now can be transformed into life-affirming and loving feelings toward yourself. You're beginning a journey of knowing that at your essence, at your core, you're love. You may need to start by building a (metaphorical) internal fire. Fire transforms and transmutes, so metaphorically there will be an inner burning as you concentrate on illuminating your authentic self. Love in action is wisdom. Both love and wisdom are inherent to your essential nature. This is what you're uncovering as you heal trauma.

STRATEGIES TO SURVIVE TRAUMA

Trauma can color your perceptions of yourself, others, and the world. The adaptations, patterns, and behaviors that you may have developed in response were necessary, your attempt to keep yourself safe, which continues into adulthood. These can include withdrawing from situations, rather than staying connected; zoning out, rather than remaining present; always being *nice*, rather than expressing how you truly feel; and attending to others' needs, while not being in touch with your own.

You learned these survival strategies in frightening situations, such as being shamed rather than accepted, hurt rather than comforted, ignored rather than listened too, left alone when feeling distressed, or not held or attuned to as you needed to be to feel safe.

Over time, these ways of being become familiar. Indeed, they *are* a normal response to embedded trauma, but when you're held in such a pattern long after the trauma is over, you remain in your traumatized self. You may sense that although familiar, these patterns are limiting, even debilitating. You may even know your strategies don't serve you, yet it doesn't feel safe to not use them. Whatever the ways you've developed to cope in response to frightening early experiences, they can be transformed.

EXERCISE: How You Cope with Developmental Trauma

Read through the following list of feelings, consequences, or strategies that arise specifically from developmental trauma. Spend some time reflecting on each one to see if it applies to you.

- Do you feel disconnected from yourself, others, or the world around you? **Yes**   **No**

- Are you disconnected from your body?   **Yes**   **No**

•	Do you tend to withdraw, or shut down emotionally?	Yes	No
•	Are you an anxious person?	Yes	No
•	Are you disconnected from your emotions?	Yes	No
•	Do you attend to the needs of others before your own?	Yes	No
•	Are you aware that you have disconnected from your own needs?	Yes	No
•	Do you pressure yourself to be nice rather than expressing how you truly feel?	Yes	No
•	Do you have difficulty with authority figures?	Yes	No
•	Do you often feel unloved or unlovable?	Yes	No
•	Is your self-esteem based on how you look?	Yes	No
•	Do you tend to take on more in life than you can manage?	Yes	No
•	Do you feel pressured much of the time?	Yes	No

Now review your answers and give them some thought. What is it like to acknowledge anything you answered yes to?

_____

_____

_____

Spend a few moments reflecting on how you might feel if any of your answers were reversed. For example, if you often feel inner pressure, imagine for a moment how differently you may feel if that pressure was no longer within you. Or, if you often experience anxiety, imagine how you would feel if that experience were no longer part of your life.

_____

_____

_____

You're on your way to revolutionizing your relationship and connection with yourself, your body, and your emotions. This vital sense of self-connection will help you respond to life in healthier ways. Through your self-connectedness, and then connectedness to others, you'll grow, heal, and develop resilience to any future trauma, and your heart will begin to fully open. With an open heart you'll find a depth of contact with yourself that you may have always desired but may not even be aware of now. There is so much wonderful and life-enhancing possibility to come for you as you work through your trauma. I'm purposely offering many *positive* possibilities. Imagining these helps you prepare your body for the more challenging aspects of healing trauma that you'll face. By encouraging your body to move toward self-organization with pleasant experiences, you become more resilient and tolerant of the less pleasant experiences you may feel in their time for resolution. Self-organization is your body's natural ability to do what it's supposed to do for balance and well-being.

INTERGENERATIONAL TRAUMA

The vast array of emotional, physical, and psychological disorders that disconnect people from their bodies, their vitality, and others may originate beyond personal experience and your family of origin. As recent epigenetic studies demonstrate, trauma and its effects can be inherited from previous generations. This *intergenerational trauma* is passed from one generation to the next. Your symptoms and difficulties with trauma could be inherited from your parents or grandparents, or even further back through collective trauma such as slavery, racism, homophobia, or war-related violence including genocide. You may inherit the memory, epigenetically (explained shortly) and psychologically. If trauma remains unresolved in your lineage, you may experience the residual effects of that trauma symptomatically much as you would with any developmental trauma.

You inherit from your parents the sequence of DNA that encodes the way your body develops and its unique characteristics. There is even a difference between the inherited trauma from mothers and fathers. Children of mothers experiencing post-traumatic stress disorder (PTSD) are at greater risk of developing PTSD, whereas children of fathers experiencing PTSD are at greater risk for serious depressive orders.[10]

The way your brain will develop is also encoded in your DNA. Your experience and your environment influence the chromosomes in your DNA, creating epigenetic changes that affect the way your genes express themselves. These changes can result in both positive adaptations and negative effects. For instance, negative effects from neglect or abuse early in your life create epigenetic changes that are not optimal for your well-being, development, and ongoing life experience. Studies show that maternal care, or lack thereof, changes the epigenetic regulation of your capacity to self-regulate.[11] Your ability to move toward self-regulation is a critical and empowering element of your healing capacity. Recovering from trauma is life changing for you, your generation, and generations to come. Your work supports a more positive future for us all.

YOUR PARENTS' AND GRANDPARENTS' TRAUMA

Reflect on what you know about your parents' and grandparents' lives. Think of any traumas you know of that they may have endured. This could be loss of a child, abortion, surviving the holocaust, surgery, war-related violence, racism, natural disaster, and more.

Use this chart to record your family trauma.

Mother	Father	Maternal Grandmother	Maternal Grandfather	Paternal Grandmother	Paternal Grandfather

It's okay if you don't have any information on family or intergenerational trauma; simply understand that intergenerational trauma does exist. The exercises you're doing address all forms of trauma and will help you bring your body back into self-organization and balance regardless of the origins.

If you did have information to record, you may experience a sense of empowerment as you look at your family history chart. Simply recognizing that the patterns you've identified as stemming from trauma may not have started with you can be a relief.

Though trauma can be carried for multiple generations, our destinies are not set in our DNA. You can resolve trauma even when you've suffered it early in your life or inherited the effects of your parents' and ancestors' trauma. You can teach your brain to decode the sensory language of tissues, organs, and body systems that experienced early emotional shaking. As you deepen your capacity to focus on your personal psychobiological awareness, you'll develop an embodied presence—calm, vibrant, grounded in your bodily experience—with a heightened capacity for the sensory attunement and resonance that may have been disrupted by that early and intergenerational or shock trauma.

Now record your responses to what you've read so far.' As you work with these self-observation and assessment exercises, you're developing your capacity to be present and to self-regulate.

_____

_____

_____

_____

_____

_____

_____

CHAPTER 2

Calming the Fight-or-Flight Response

Wouldn't it be nice to feel truly comfortable and present in your body—to be attuned to its needs and its signals in a congruent, loving, and respectful rapport? Wouldn't it be wonderful to be calm and present to your emotions and feelings, fully aware of life's myriad expressions, moment to moment—love, grief, sadness, joy—to allow these human expressions to flow through you, to not deny them. Your relationship with your body is reciprocal. As you learn to listen and respond to its needs, it will bring you clarity and wisdom that can enhance all aspects of your life. Like any relationship, where there may have been some difficulties and challenges it takes time to heal, to cultivate a depth of understanding and a loving affinity, but it's possible.

Wherever you may be on this path of healing and embodiment, as you restore your body/mind from the impact of trauma, it's essential to revisit safety in your body—or to start feeling safe for the first time. No matter how long after the original trauma, experiencing safety is the cornerstone for growth. Feelings of safety hold you from the inside out. They allow you to experience a deeper connection to your body, to others, and to the world around you. Cultivating islands of safety is the best way for you to support yourself as possibly difficult or unfamiliar emotions, feelings, and energies arise. Safety and body awareness become allies, allowing your body/mind to naturally approach the inherent wisdom that moves you toward healing.

In this chapter you'll learn how to nurture safety in your body. Neurobiological research reveals the importance of safety to your ability to be connected,[12] and this chapter is rich with preparatory skills to help you ameliorate the pervasive nature of trauma, while cultivating your capacity for presence, connection, and safety. The greater your sense of safety, the more you'll be able to control the more primitive survival responses of fight, flight, and freeze. Without access to feelings of safety, your survival physiology may be screaming for you to run and freeze simultaneously. Imagine you're riding a horse—your life force—and you command it to gallop *and* stop at the same time. It's internally confusing and exhausting, making it difficult to determine what may be a threat and how to appropriately respond.

If, as a child, you experienced limited safety, connection, and nurturance with your care-givers *and* in social groups, as an adult you may have limited capacity to differentiate between threat and safety. It's as if your sensors that should tell you whether someone is safe or unsafe are distorted. As a child, you needed consistent access to safety to encode that sense of safety within you, for your neuroceptive systems (perception that lies beneath your conscious aware-ness) to develop in ways that allow you to recognize actual safety or threat. This distortion may be slight or exaggerated. Once you create internal safety, your neuroception will begin to shift toward greater accuracy.

Healing trauma isn't about *getting back into your body*. It's about addressing and healing why you disconnected from it in the first place. Initiating islands of safety within you can open a doorway for connection.

ISLANDS OF SAFETY

When you anchor a feeling of safety in your body and *really* have the felt sense experience of it—even just a small island of safety—your body becomes familiar enough for you to be able to return to it. When your system senses safety, you're neurologically supported for connection and regulation. You'll even help regulate others, as your voice, facial expressions, and eyes will convey that safety.[13]

Because safety is a vital component in your healing, it's essential to take time to practice and deepen the skills that enhance safety. All your body awareness explorations invite the organic and intuitive aspect of your body to join your mind's logic and rationality, enhancing your inherent wisdom. The images you encounter through healing will also connect your bodily experience and your mind. These images signal new neural connections and will help guide your emergent growth process.

EXERCISE: Feeling Safe

In this exercise you'll use your imagination to create a person or place that feels safe, then anchor that feeling in your body to begin the *feeling safe within* process. Read over the exercise first, then take your time as you go through it.

1. Sit in a comfortable place and position. Take a few moments to think about where and when you feel safe. Be creative. It might be a place in nature, a favorite room in your home, snuggled up in bed with a favorite blanket, feeling your breath move in your body, being with a loved one, or imagining a spiritual figure holding or protecting you in some way.

2. Imagine you're in your safe place or have your safe object or person close by. Notice what happens in your body. Try this in your actual safe place if you can.

3. See if you can locate any sensations connected with your body that are associated with images of safety. Images are a powerful means of transformation.

4. Look for any places where your body may feel warmer, slightly relaxed, more open, softer, or more expansive, or your breath is deepening even slightly.

5. Can you describe what safety feels like? Record your responses here or in your journal.

6. Maybe nothing feels safe in your body yet. In this case, what feels less scary, less difficult, or less tight in your body?

_____

_____

_____

As you become more familiar with this sense of safety, remember to be on the lookout for times in your day-to-day life where you notice feeling safe, or at least *less unsafe*. Then be curious and consider:

I feel safe, or less anxious, or less numb. How do I know I'm feeling this way?

Where in my body do I feel safe?

The sensations of feeling safe are . . .

Safety is not the absence of threat, but a feeling experience that you're cultivating within your body to allow connection to happen naturally.

ACTIVATING YOUR CAPACITY FOR EXPANSION AND CONTRACTION

Healing from trauma isn't so much about being able to relax as it is about being able to tolerate a wide range of emotional, physical, mental, relational, and spiritual experiences, with increased awareness and conscious presence (without becoming overwhelmed). This entails a back-and-forth movement between an experience of inner contraction of your body and an experience of inner expansion or spaciousness. As you experience the feelings of inner expansion—as if space is opening within you, which can feel quite lovely—your physiology may unravel itself from the physiological constriction and possibly immobility that is a natural reaction to a perceived threat. But contraction and expansion is also a natural rhythm when trauma isn't present. Within the sense of inner spaciousness that you'll discover, your physiology can shift into an overall experience of reorganization—your body moving toward its innate and optimal capacity for wisdom and healing. Initially you may not notice the feelings of expansion, even when you begin to feel less uncomfortable; however, as your body awareness and sense of safety deepen, you'll experience this. The experience of expansion can be delightful, and the experience of contraction restful, renewing, and soft, rather than disengaging and disconnecting.

The trauma cycle disrupts this intrinsic rhythm of contraction and expansion, which gets stuck in the contracted or constricted survival mode. As you initiate the movement back and forth between pleasant and unpleasant experiences, you're stimulating your natural rhythm to once again establish itself.

EXERCISE: Stimulating Your Body's Natural Rhythm

(An audio recording of instructions for this exercise is available at http://www.newharbinger .com/43256.)

Part 1:

1. Sit or lie down in a comfortable position.

2. Recall a very pleasant experience from any time in your life. Stay connected to the memory for a few minutes.

3. As you remember, do you notice any pleasant change in your body or have a pleasant image?

4. Do you notice a sense of softening, expansion, or spaciousness in your body?

5. If not, return to this exercise once you have a deeper connection with your body and its sensations.

Part 2:

1. Next, recall an unpleasant time in your life. Don't go to your worst memory; choose one that creates a very slight tensing or contraction in your body. Observe this for a few moments. Be curious how your body changes, even slightly.

2. Go back to the pleasant scenario for a couple of minutes. Anchor the pleasant feelings.

3. Now go back to the unpleasant experience. Then return to the pleasant experience.

4. Go back and forth between these experiences a few times. Even if it's very slight, you'll have a direct experience of expansion and contraction that will grow over time.

Record what you noticed in your body during this exercise.

_____

_____

_____

The following story of Jonathan offers an example of a shock trauma and how easy it is to override your body's signals and move on with life.

WHEN THE IMPACT OF SHOCK CREATES TRAUMA

Jonathan was driving to a baseball game one sunny Sunday afternoon. As he drew close to the sports arena, the traffic became heavier. He reached to turn down the music so he could better concentrate on driving. In that instant, a car rear-ended him. The airbag deployed, hitting him hard in the chest as his head whipped forward and back with the impact. He went into shock immediately. Jonathan got out of his car and stumbled around, dazed and confused, unable to make sense of what had happened. People who had stopped and gotten out of their cars came toward him and asked him to sit down. As he did, his body started to tremble. This frightened him even more. He intentionally stopped the trembling by trying to *pull himself together*, to orient to where he was and what had happened.

With the help of police officers who arrived on the scene, it took about twenty minutes before Jonathan could feel some sort of return to a "normal," pre-accident state. He called a friend to come and drive him home. Although he returned to his everyday life without much thought of the accident, Jonathan began to experience moments of disconnection and feeling dazed, fearful, anxious, and angry. It was difficult for him to make any sense of what was happening to him. His body was stuck in a survival mode of contraction and fear. He eventually sought professional help to support him in resolving his symptoms, whose effects had remained with him weeks after the initial shock of the event.

It was fortunate that Jonathan sought professional help. For some individuals, symptoms of trauma don't emerge for months or years after the traumatic event, or they simply don't connect their symptoms with trauma and instead find ways to repress or override their body's distress. An overwhelming event—such as a car accident, a fall, an emotional blow, or sudden natural disaster, a rape and other unexpected abuse—is often referred to as an acute or shock trauma. Acute trauma occurs when you experience an unexpected and very frightening event that jolts you. In addition to the physical injuries you may suffer, this shock directly affects your nervous system. It's difficult to grasp or absorb the significance of this type of traumatic event in the moment. If you've experienced a shock trauma you were probably left feeling dazed, confused, and fearful to some degree.

For Jonathan, anger at the person who rear-ended him remained unintegrated until he received somatic (learning to sense the body) and psychological help. In addition to disconnecting the anger, Jonathan also remained disconnected from his body.

The impact was far too quick for his body's natural motor response for protection at the time of the accident. In therapy, Jonathan eventually completed the motor movements his body needed to make in response to the impact, such as putting his hands up to protect his face. As he did this, his body gently trembled, and the traumatic energy diminished. His body softened and relaxed in the realization that the threat was over and he was now safe.

Memory is not only emotional and cognitive; it resides in the body, too. Unfinished physical impacts of trauma can remain held in your body. Body awareness and the somatic interventions that address them must be used to integrate shock traumas.[14] You'll find many ways to do this throughout this workbook.

RESOLVING THE RESPONSE

After a shock trauma, it's natural for your body to shake or tremble. Trembling is a physiological survival response, a release of life force energy meant to allow your body to return to homeostasis—your normal baseline of balance.

When the traumatic event is over and the threat has passed, if you haven't run or fought, the excess energy can dissipate naturally if you allow trembling and spontaneous deep breaths. However, the natural state of trembling or shaking may feel frightening. People describe it as having no control of their body, which can feel very scary. If you don't know that this trembling is a healthy response, you may stop or override it, or simply not notice it as you disconnect from your body.

Until that survival energy is discharged and/or integrated into your body, the energy will remain trapped within you. This may contribute to dysregulation in many of your bodily systems, such as your immune system. It can also impair your emotional and social capacities. For instance, you may feel emotionally numb or in a constant state of vigilance, or lose interest in connecting with others. Other symptoms include anxiety, depression, panic, intrusive thoughts, and headaches.

By reconnecting with the life force energy that remains bound within you after trauma, you're optimizing your capacity for healing and growth.

PAUSE FOR REFLECTION: Your Personal Experience
of Discharging Traumatic Energy

- Have you ever experienced shaking or trembling after a traumatic event?   **Yes**   **No**

- If yes, how did you respond to the trembling?

  _____

- If it was uncomfortable, would you be more comfortable now,
  knowing it's a healthy response to shock?   **Yes**   **No**

- When you tune in to your body, do you sometimes experience trembling? What is that like for you?

  _____

EXERCISE: A Time for Calm

Reading about trauma and working on recognizing and releasing its lasting effects can be quite a tumultuous experience. Any time you begin to feel overwhelmed, or if you notice trembling that begins to feel too much, pause and return to your grounding exercises. You now have more capacity to face fear than you did during the trauma that was so understandably fear-inducing. Anytime you're feeling unsettled, use the following exercise to help you find some calmness. Keep it in your repertoire of calming and healing skills.

1. Rub your hands together, using friction to create warmth in your hands.

2. Place your hands on your heart.

3. Feel the warmth and the slight pressure of your touch.

4. Imagine you're breathing in and out of your heart where your hands are.

5. Invoke a sense of calm, compassion, or love; feel your breath moving that quality through your whole heart and chest area. If you cannot immediately generate that feeling, use your imagination to help evoke it.

6. Practice this breath of calm, compassion, or love for a few minutes.

7. Notice any changes you experience.

8. Write about your experience in this exercise, using the language of sensation and emotion.

    _____

    _____

    _____

This exercise is a wonderful way to bring yourself a sense of calm and safety. Research shows that the heart, like the brain, has its own network of neural cells that communicate directly with your brain. Your caring intent and warm touch swiftly activate the release of oxytocin—the brain hormone that brings feelings of safety, trust, bonding, and calm.

KNOWING YOUR BODY'S INNATE FLOW OF DEFENSE MECHANISMS

Did you know that the first innate defense mechanism when you perceive danger is staying connected to others? This is humans' most evolved defense. Connection with others who are safe, with whom we can engage, allows us to stay present even during a crisis or traumatic event. Of course, in a frightening situation there may not be someone close by who is safe. Sometimes the person who is meant to be safe is actually hurting you. Your next line of defense is to call for help. This response is connected to your sympathetic nervous system (SNS) and the panic circuits of your brain. If no one *safe* arrives, your innate flow of defenses then prepares you to flee. In this state of hyperarousal, the fear circuits of your brain are recruited to help you get out of the situation.[15]

During a severe traumatic event, the activation of the fear response shuts down 80 to 90 percent of the brain's function.[16] It's very confusing and frightening when you cannot access your usual brain functioning. The next line of defense if you cannot flee to safety is the fight response, in which the anger circuits of your brain are activated. In this *hyperaroused* state, your heart rate, respiration, and blood pressure elevate. The hyperarousal induces a cascade of released stress hormones.

Often a traumatic impact happens so quickly that, like Jonathan in his car accident, you're unable to respond with any of these innate defenses, and they may remain stuck within you. If you cannot act on your instinctual mobilizing responses of fight or flight, and you cannot reach safety, your next resort is the *freeze* response. Your muscle tone is rigid; your eyes may dart around scanning for danger and escape routes, looking for possible lifesaving actions. However, if you cannot act, and the fear continues, your energy-saving parasympathetic nervous system (PNS) is triggered into action, creating a state of *hypoarousal*, or immobility, with lowered heart rate and blood pressure and slower respiration along with the release of pain-numbing endogenous opioids—should the threat be fatal, these make death more painless.[17]

This switch from a fearful, anxious, or angry state to immobility stems from your internal evaluation that the impending danger cannot be avoided. Feeling completely helpless in the face of danger, perceiving no way to escape, you have no choice: you *involuntarily* surrender to this immobilized state. This is one of the most ancient defense mechanisms of our autonomic nervous system (ANS). When your system abandons fight or flight, it's trying to save your life; the immobility response is an energy-saving response (in animals it's known as a *death-feigning response*). Those awful feelings of helplessness and powerlessness you may experience as part of your trauma symptoms are often an outcome of unresolved immobility (more on this in the next chapter).

To recap your body's innate flow of defenses:

- Social engagement. Connection to others for safety. Your most evolved defense.

- Cry for help. To mobilize a stronger or wiser other for help.

- Flight. Mobilizing defense. Experiencing fear.

- Fight. Mobilizing defense. Experiencing anger.

- Freeze. Frozen with fear. Immobilizing defense. Feeling paralyzed, yet the eyes can scan.

- Shutdown or collapse. Immobilizing defense. The most primitive defense. Cannot orient to the environment. Can experience helplessness, loss of movement, loss of awareness.

You can get stuck in any of these defense mechanisms; they remain active within you, yet you can manage to move on in life. Fortunately, you have mechanisms that protect your heart and brain form shutting down at several levels in the body.[18] Could there be a thwarted response of flight or fight in your body? It may feel at times that you are

- Ready to bolt for the door, or feeling like you want to run away, even though the situation doesn't really call for any action like that

- Hypervigilant, unsafe, angry and defensive, aggressive or impulsive, or highly reactive

- Often clenching your hands and jaw

- Experiencing a lot of body tension and constriction

Describe your experience of any of these that you relate to. It's important for you to become aware of any *hyperaroused* state, such as hypervigilance, or *hyporaroused* state, such as immobility or shutting down. As you explore and describe, notice your body experience, how you feel as you acknowledge and develop more body awareness. To monitor these states and become more familiar with them, keep returning to the orienting and grounding exercises, to help you consolidate and integrate your gains at deeper levels. Be curious about sensations, emotions, images, perceptions, and memories. Write these down as you notice them.

_____

_____

_____

_____

Chronic SNS activation is very hard on your body, especially if you tend to also disconnect from your body. You'll be addressing this shortly, and you may begin to feel empowered as you realize that some of these often-odd experiences are part of the trauma response you are healing.

CHANGING THE TERRIBLE IMAGES OF YOUR TRAUMA

Your imaginative capacities can support your healing in many ways. Functional imaging studies of the brain have shown that imagining a movement activates a motor network that intersects with the networks involved when you're performing the actual movement. For example, your brain responds to *imagining* you're running or fighting to escape danger much as it does to your physically doing those things.

Using your imagination to complete the defenses, such as running or fighting your way to safety, completes the cycle, which resolves that innate response to trauma. This is a safe and powerful way to use your imagination for trauma resolution.

Ginette Paris describes this process wonderfully; "By re-imaging the object of my fear, the bear appears on the footpath. I can then find the proper action: run from it, fight with it, take it to the zoo, tame it, or avoid the path that crosses its lair."[19]

Using your imagination, make certain that *this* time you triumph in the situation and find your way to safety. Remember, your first innate defensive response is social engagement with another. This inborn psychophysiological organization system helps you regulate yourself.[20]

A cautionary note: Begin with less extreme traumatic events. Over time, as you increase resilience, you can work with more intense scenarios. If you've experienced severely traumatizing events like a rape or other sexual or physical abuse, or shock, I strongly recommend you work with a therapist for your safety. The energetic and emotional components will be very intense.

As you practice these exercises, you may feel the unresolved survival energy moving in your body, as tingling, trembling, or heat. This is your body reregulating itself as you integrate and/or release life force energy. Pause and observe your body as you notice changes.

Also, when you reimagine your response to that "bear," you don't have to be alone! You can bring in another person or ally (such as a knight, angel or deity) to help you "find the proper action" and carry it out. There are three options for this in the next, three-part exercise.

EXERCISE: Completing Innate Defense Responses

The first part is for any time you've experienced a frightening event and wanted someone to comfort you. The second is for times when you wanted to run away and couldn't. The third is for times you wanted to fight but couldn't.

Part 1: Kind Eyes and a Loving Embrace

Recall a traumatic or frightening event when you needed someone safe to hold and soothe you and this didn't happen. *This time* you'll change the experience to a positive one.

For example: Mary Ellen remembered a time when her mother was extremely late to pick her up from school. She was four years old. She stood alone outside the school gates, waiting, very scared. Her mother arrived, stressed. She missed seeing how scared her daughter was. As they drove home, Mary Ellen sat in the back seat, still in a dazed state. She chose this event to work with and heal. When she recalled the memory, she imagined her mother smiling as she got out of the car, holding her, telling her everything was fine and that she loved her. As she imagined, Mary Ellen paid close attention to her body, which began to shift as she felt the comfort from her mother. Her breathing deepened, her shoulders relaxed, and she felt as if that old memory of being scared dissolved from her body.

1. Find a comfortable place to sit and notice how you feel.

2. Notice what changes as you recall the frightening event.

3. Rather than remember it as it happened, recreate the scene, being met with kind and loving eyes or a soothing embrace. Be creative! And remember to notice your body as you imagine.

Part 2: Running to Safety, Kind Eyes, and a Loving Embrace

Do you remember a time when you felt you would have liked to run from danger but couldn't? If so, you're going to give yourself the corrective experience of running to safety. When you get to safety, see a loving face with kind eyes as you receive a loving embrace. Be as creative and kind to yourself as possible.

For example: John's father came home one evening in a drunken state and began shouting at him. John was terrified. He wanted to run but felt frozen. As John renegotiated the memory, when his father began to shout, John ran to his aunt's house. She held him and looked at him lovingly as she told him he was safe.

1. Find a comfortable place to sit.

2. Notice your body as you begin to contemplate the event.

3. Create the scene in which you can run. As you see yourself running, feel your body, especially your legs. You may feel energy moving through you as if you're actually running. Run as much as you need to. Now find a person who's safe and has kind and loving eyes or can hold you in a loving, soothing embrace.

4. Feel your body as much as possible; feel any pleasant or softening sensations and emotions. Notice if you take a deep breath; feel the long exhalation.

5. Rest for a few minutes, then describe how the experience was for you.

_____

_____

_____

Part 3: Fighting Back to Get to Safety, Kind Eyes, and a Loving Embrace

Do you remember a time when you would have liked to fight back in a situation to get to safety? Anger is the primary emotion of the fight response—the emotion derived from the activation of your SNS, energizing your body to fend off danger.

For example, Anna's big brother used to sit on her and pinch her. Her brother was bigger, and she could never escape. This was not fun for Anna. It was too much, and it made her very angry. In her reimagining, she found she couldn't fight him off alone, so she imagined an angel as an ally who helped give her the strength to push him off of her. Then she ran to her mother, who comforted her.

1. Find a comfortable place to sit.

2. Contemplate the event in which you'd have liked to fight back.

3. Imagine the scene in which you *can* fight back. Feel your body; allow it to tell you what it would like to do to fight. Push the person away, kick, hit, bite—whatever you need to do. See yourself clearly winning and then getting away.

4. After fighting, you may need to run to a safe place, or a safe person may come to you.

5. Then find a person who's safe and has kind and loving eyes or can give you a loving, soothing embrace.

6. As you do this, feel your body as much as possible. Notice any energy moving through your body; stay present with this. Notice any pleasant sensations and emotions.

7. Describe how the experience was for you.

_____

_____

_____

8. Now describe your relationship with your body and your imagination after working through this chapter. Describe any insights you had about your life force moving through you. Although you weren't working with any aspect that directly addressed spirituality, on the continuum of healing, spirituality is about connection. In which ways do you feel more connected? Do you feel safer, or more connected to your body? To your being?

_____

_____

_____

_____

As powerful as it can feel to complete innate defenses with your imagination, this is only a part of healing trauma. As you continue in the workbook, you'll keep addressing the patterns, adaptations, and erroneous beliefs that no longer serve you. Developmental trauma and shock trauma need to be addressed differently. You may find that you transition from working with a shock trauma and completing an innate defense response, to fulfilling what was absent in your early years—an absence that felt so threatening that trauma emerged within you.

Before moving on to the next chapter, let's take some time to learn about and explore more ways you can support yourself and enhance your life.

CREATING YOUR RESOURCE INVENTORY

A resource could be a person, a pet, eating with a friend, sitting in nature, practicing yoga, sipping a cup of tea—the possibilities are endless. Resources facilitate a positive experience that will help you develop layers of resilience in your nervous system—vital to healing and preventing trauma symptoms in any future potentially traumatic event.

Thinking of or connecting to a resource can stimulate a calming response. Your resources are a reminder to your ANS of its innate capacity for self-regulation—your ability to return to your baseline of inner balance, and one of the key elements of healing.

Here are some resource examples.

Internal Resources

- Your imagination; for instance, imagine lying on a hammock on the beach, feeling the soothing rocking motion, feeling the warmth of the sun on your skin, listening to the sound of the waves.

- Your sense of humor; laughter *is* the best medicine! It helps you embrace the spontaneous nature of life.

- Meditation; for example, following the sensations of your breath, or expressing gratitude.

External Resources

- The love or comfort you feel when you're with pets or other animals

- Friends, family, community

- Eating with others (research shows this increases happiness)

- Nature, exercising, creative expressions such as dance, yoga, singing, art, music, and so on

As you heal, you'll discover infinite resources. For a resource to be truly effective, connect it with your body—feel the sensations produced in your body by your resource. Perhaps you feel calm when you hold your dog, or your eyes soften when you look at art, or you feel enthusiastic (which creates a feeling of expansion) when you're in nature. See if you can name the sensation: is it relaxing, soothing, softening, expansive? The more you can feel the calming sensations that emerge in response to your resource, the more resilience you're developing. Resilience supports your body/mind system in restoring and maintaining balance and systemic organization—a state of feeling at ease, curious, open, and creative.

For some people who've suffered a great deal of trauma, initially it may be difficult to notice any pleasant sensations. Sometimes, and maybe for a while, nothing seems to feel good. In this case, notice what feels *less* painful or not so difficult. Every small step is a step toward full recovery.

Be creative in identifying resources. They can be transitory, such as a colorful orchid that you bring into your home, or long-term, like a piece of art or a friendship. A resource can be a monthly meeting with friends or a soothing or invigorating morning ritual—lighting a candle, expressing a body-centered prayer.

Once you've created your resource list, you'll focus on your experience of body awareness and deepen into the less difficult and more pleasant, softening, or calming sensations your resources evoke. This will ignite your innate *organizing* capacity—that is, your body's natural ability to do what it's supposed to do, while allowing you to stay in the present moment. It's your body's inherent wisdom. You're reminding your ANS, which is key in healing trauma, of its inherent ability for self-regulation.

YOUR RESOURCES

Compile a table of your current resources. Keep adding to it whenever you discover things that help you return to a more relaxed and balanced state.

RESOURCES YOU'D LIKE TO CREATE

Here, record the resources that you would like to create in your life, both internal and external; for instance, dinner with friends once a month, practicing yoga or meditation, beginning an art class, taking up martial arts, active imagination.

Internal Resources	External Resources

CHAPTER 3

Identifying Patterns of Dissociation to Regain Your Vitality

Faced with danger and filled with fear, seeing no means of escape, you may have *surrendered* to the immobility response without conscious choice. In such a scenario, dissociation comes with the release of pain-numbing endogenous opioids—your body's natural pain killers. It's nature's gift for mammals to feel less of the unbearableness of trauma, and in case of death, to make it less painful.

This chapter will help you to understand and normalize the process of dissociation and immobility and to identify any shutdown or dissociative responses within you. Because dissociation disconnects many elements of your being—such as emotions, feelings, images, and thoughts—throughout the workbook you'll develop practices that gently reconnect these elements. You'll explore the relationship between your body, intense emotions, and immobility or dissociation, along with your relationship to spirituality, life force, and intellect.

THE ESSENCE OF TRAUMA

Bessel van der Kolk, a psychiatrist and expert on post-traumatic stress, identifies dissociation as the essence of our response to trauma.[21] Dissociation, if time-limited, is a healthy adaptive response. It's as if a switch connecting you to your body is turned off and you move into a state of internal disconnection, which prevents you from feeling what you perceive as intolerable. Psychiatrist Frank Putnam called dissociation "the escape when there is no escape."[22]

However, if this dissociative state is prolonged, your fundamental world view becomes distorted. In a continued dissociative state, you may miss the signs when danger is present. Or you may inaccurately detect danger where there is none. You could say your body is still scared, even though you *know* the actual danger is over. The experience of being dissociated varies widely—from mild feelings of detachment, to more severe disconnection, to further psycho-pathological dissociation that involves dissociative disorders. If you suspect you may have a dissociative disorder, talk to a medical professional, as your initial healing may be beyond the scope of this book.

With dissociation you may feel disoriented, unreal, a bit spacey, confused, or just *different* at times, though you can't quite name why. You may also drift off into your own world or be consumed by a totally different task than the one at hand, or you can become clumsy, bump into things, and be unresponsive to your immediate environment. You realize you're disconnected from your body and emotions, unable to adequately feel them. Many people know they are dissociated but they aren't able to reconnect or integrate their experience without help.

Some of my patients report dissociation as a pleasant feeling; others are frightened by it. You may be aware that dissociation comes and goes, depending on what is happening in your life. Here is how Frank experienced it.

FRANK'S STORY

When my client Frank, a man who had practiced martial arts most of his life, was held up by two men on the street, one wielding a small knife, he froze in terror. His body became numb, and he felt distant from the frightening scene. Afterward, he loathed himself for what he called his *stupidity*, and he felt deeply ashamed, knowing he could have disarmed the men with his martial arts skill and strength. However, as Frank and I discovered in our trauma healing sessions together, Frank had endured a physically abusive childhood, which affected his capacity to mobilize as an adult in the face of threat.

As a child, Frank often felt terrified when his father raged. As he feared the worst, and with no way to flee or fight, his system would automatically shift into the defensive response of dissociation, immobility, and shutdown. This, plus overwhelming experiences of *terror, anger,* and *shame*, and negative thoughts such as *I'm unlovable*, created a psychological and physiological circuit breaker that could be tripped at any time, leading to dissociation.

In the holdup, Frank's body perceived no way to escape. This level of perception, called *neuroception*, detects risk beneath your conscious awareness.[23] Faced with a threat, Frank's body neurocepted the same danger he'd experienced as a child and reacted similarly—he froze, disconnected, and shut down, powerless over his body. This is very common in trauma; neural nets of remembering the past are experienced as happening *now*, especially if something related to the original event is sensed in the moment.

Understanding that feelings of helplessness are often a part of the dissociative state, consider your own experience. Do you ever find yourself feeling hopeless, powerless, or frozen in fear when there is no obvious threat and the response doesn't make sense? If so, are you beginning to sense what may trigger those feelings?

Dissociation is a sacrifice of the unity of the self that emerges from the depths of helplessness, a profoundly distressing experience that may continue to live within you. Whenever you notice you are dissociating or are heading into an immobility or shutdown response, it's important to begin carefully mobilizing your energy. The following exercise can help.

EXERCISE: Beginning to Shift Out of Feeling Helpless

These simple actions give your prefrontal cortex (your executive functioning) a chance to take over and stop a trauma response. Use them in the midst of any triggering situation to interrupt the response and reconnect to your body.

1. Rub your hands together.

2. Move your body in some way—stand up, gently shake your arms and legs, jump up and down and jiggle your body—to get your life force moving.

3. Reconnect to your body and notice what you feel after moving.

4. Orient to the space around you, moving your head, neck, and eyes. Notice your breath.

5. After your first run-through to try out the exercise, record what you observe:

    _____

    _____

    _____

SITUATIONS THAT CAN TRIGGER IMMOBILITY

The instinctual immobility response, also known as a *shutdown state*, occurs in a variety of threatening situations when the body perceives fear and no way to escape—situations including sexual assault, childhood sexual abuse, and childhood neglect. This response can also be catalyzed in acute traumas that severely shock the body/mind, such as car accidents, falls, surgeries, emotional distress, and loss.

It's important to understand immobility as an essential response of our body, brain, and trauma because when you understand what is happening in your body, without your control, you can be compassionate with yourself. Shame and guilt often accompany the experience of the immobility response.[24] By appreciating it as an involuntary reflex response, you can learn that the inability to react was not your fault, and reduce the wretched feelings of shame and guilt. (We'll explore more about shame in upcoming chapters.)

EXERCISE: Identifying Patterns of Dissociation

Perhaps you're aware, or are becoming more aware, of the way you experience dissociation. Use the following questions to bring more awareness to this experience.

- Are you aware that you have a pattern of dissociating or feeling like you emotionally or physically shut down in stressful situations?   Yes   No

- Are you aware that you dissociate, but are unsure what triggers the dissociation?   Yes   No

- If you're aware that you dissociate, do you know what triggers it? If yes, describe here.

_____

_____

- In challenging situations, do you feel spacey or dazed?   Yes   No

- Do you stare fixedly, not really looking at anything?   Yes   No

- Do you zone out easily?   Yes   No

- When asked to notice your body, do you zone out?   Yes   No

- Do you disconnect from your body and become intellectual in order to not feel?   Yes   No

- Do you tend to become overly spiritual in challenging situations? For example, do you invest a spiritual meaning in situations that relieves you from the tension? Or do you impart a spiritual nature to a situation and focus on that to avoid feeling numb? (You may need to reflect on this for a while.)   **Yes   No**

- Do you disappear into your mind or thinking capacities to avoid feeling?   **Yes   No**

- Considering how many Yes answers you circled, do you have any other insights about your patterns of dissociation? Describe them. If you find you are judging yourself in any way, remember that these patterns initially emerged to protect you.

  _____

  _____

  _____

  _____

  _____

The impact of a shock trauma can trigger an *expansion of consciousness*, which can feel quite pleasant, somewhat safe and painless, yet it is disconnected from the body. This prevents the person from reconnecting to the body. The shock, energy, and emotions would be overwhelming, so the person stays within the expansion, but the trauma doesn't get resolved. This is also dissociation, similar to the phenomenon of *death-feigning*, where a part of your consciousness may be in a state between life and death. Your work is to make your body a safe place again, so your consciousness can fully return to it.

Psychiatrist Iain McGilchrist says that the protective defense of dissociation feels like a "psychic death and an inability to sustain a sense of inner aliveness."[25] It's this inner aliveness, so often deadened in trauma, that you're going to reestablish. Whether you were traumatized as an infant, child, or adult, you use tremendous amounts of energy to keep disconnected—to keep unbearable feelings, sensations, and emotions outside of your conscious awareness.[26] In healing from trauma, you'll reconnect to your life force to regain your full vitality.

EXERCISE: Exploring Your Dissociative Responses

I tend to dissociate when _____

_____

_____

Dissociation feels like _____

_____

_____

Do you withdraw rather than engaging with others in certain situations? For example, in intimate, conflicting, social or emotional situations, you may find yourself wanting to be alone or withdraw to your computer. Rather than socializing with friends or colleagues, you isolate yourself, even though you would like to be more social. Describe any similar scenarios you remember.

_____

_____

_____

I become intellectual or spiritual to avoid feeling when _____

_____

_____

I find myself zoning out when _____

_____

_____

CONTINUING YOUR SAFE EMERGENCE FROM IMMOBILITY

Underlying the immobility and shutdown response is a huge amount of energy and unexpressed emotion—often anger or rage. These powerful emotions and energy can frighten anyone. You may or may not be aware of them. Whatever you couldn't feel at the time of the trauma is repressed and disconnected from your awareness. Yet when you slowly develop tolerance for experiencing what was once forgotten, and you cultivate your capacity to feel intense emotion, you can experience an embodiment that allows vitality to emerge once again and fill your body.

In the resolution process, as you unearth feelings related to trauma, it's important to not revive these intense emotions too soon or all at once in a sudden catharsis. Carl Jung explained: "It forces itself tyrannically upon the conscious mind. The explosion of affect is a complete invasion of the individual. It pounces upon him like an enemy or a wild animal."[27] This is a very intense and scary experience. You may have experienced this phenomenon; it's terrifying to be flooded by a wave of intense emotion. The intention throughout this workbook is to prevent this and keep you safe in your explorations and integration of your body, life force, and emotions.

Fortunately, the survival response embedded in trauma can catalyze spiritual transformation. The energy of anger, rage, and other survival life force energy can be beneficial when you allow your body to express its natural connection to spiritual transformation.

As you become more aware of this energy and its movement within your body, your body may move into archetypal gestures, or mudras, portraying elements of the spiritual aspect of your healing process. If you find slow movements of your hands or body happening, feel the gesture inwardly, asking yourself *how does this feel within*? These movements are not dramatic but have a distinct mystical quality of the numinous, and you may feel the sacredness of the moment in a quiet spaciousness opening up within you. In these instances of inner focus and awareness you can access the riches of your inner resources on your path of embodied trauma resolution. You'll be exploring this more in upcoming chapters.

DEEPENING YOUR CONNECTION TO YOUR BODY

You can practice the following exercise at any time. It can begin the day gently, tenderly acknowledging your body. It allows you to deeply feel your body in time and space, silently accepting it as a supportive place to be.

In this exercise, you'll use proprioception to enhance your body awareness. The proprioceptors are specialized sensory receptors on nerve endings in your muscles, tendons, and joints that relay information about your position and movement to keep you oriented to your body position and movement in space. Proprioceptors detect subtle changes in body movement, position, tension, and force, and the brain interprets and responds to this data. The more you practice, the more body awareness you'll have. If you practice the exercise like a moving meditation, it will enhance your overall awareness and bring a sense of relaxation and calm. Many have found it helpful to break patterns of intrusive thoughts or negative thinking.

EXERCISE: Finding Your Body in Time and Space

Preparation:

Read the entire exercise before you begin. The idea is to place your attention in each joint as you move them in a variety of directions. Don't go beyond what feels comfortable to you. If you have distinct joint discomfort, try micromovements. Enjoy the simplicity of this exercise and the gift of simply being present to your body and feeling into the joints as much as you can.

1. Sit in a comfortable chair and remove your shoes and socks.

2. Begin to slowly stretch and curl your toes in every direction.

3. Be aware of the toe joints. Feel, or imagine you can feel, the space between the bones as you move them. Spend about two minutes doing this.

4. Continue moving your joints and bringing your awareness to the space between the bones as you move to your

5. Ankles

6. Knees

7. Fingers

8. Wrists

9. Elbows

10. Shoulders

11. Once you've felt all your joints moving, sit with your spine straight. Gently rotate to the left, rotating slowly upward through the spine, all the way up to your head. Feel, or imagine you can feel, each vertebra as you rotate your spine. Repeat on your right side.

12. Sitting with your spine straight, explore the sensations at the top of your spine (where your neck and head meet, just below the skull), as you make tiny little movements, as if balancing your head on top of your top vertebra.

13. Now pause and be still and simply notice your present experience, especially any sensations in your body. Allow any slow spontaneous movements your body makes to occur.

14. Was this a pleasant experience? If yes, how so? Did you feel more in touch with your body? If yes, what was that like? Record your answers and anything else you'd like to about your experience.

_____

_____

_____

PROTECTIVE STRATEGIES THAT CIRCUMVENT RESOLVING TRAUMA

Unresolved trauma can lock you in a paradox of pain. The more you avoid the past pain, the more suffering you're likely to endure over time. Most people develop adaptations and tactics that *seem* helpful to get through the trauma yet get in the way of healing. These tactics may help you feel you can survive the difficulties. In early childhood trauma, the child's brain regulatory structures haven't developed the needed integrative capacity for resolution. Both children and adults may lack the emotional or cognitive skills needed for integration. However, at some point it's better to tolerate degrees of difficulties and discomfort for a greater purpose—your authentic life and vitality.

Working hard, studying, or entering into spiritual practice are common unconscious strategies to avoid a painful past. This seems preferable to confronting the trauma, yet it ultimately destroys your quality of life. This behavior can be called *bypassing*.

Spiritual Bypassing

When reflecting on spirituality as related to resolving trauma, it's important to know a potential pitfall (especially if you have a pattern of dissociation) and how unresolved trauma can keep you from a full connection between your body and your spirituality.

When we desire to get past suffering, spirituality can itself become an unconscious means of survival to avoid the pain of trauma—a flight from unbearable experience in the body. *Spiritual bypassing* can be used to escape from aggressive impulses, fear, sorrow, despair, and the debilitating body symptoms of trauma. In early life, traumatizing conditions—whether a toxic womb, a difficult birth, surgery, neglect, anxious parents, or myriad other possibilities— can create constriction in the body, coinciding with an expansion of awareness, which catapults you out of your body and into the more energetic realms. This form of dissociation brings you to a place of seeming safety, which can be negative and positive. For instance, if you've experienced spiritual bypassing, it certainly saved you from feeling unbearable emotions, and you may have some deep and valid spiritual realizations over your lifetime, yet your connection to what feels spiritual may support your dissociation and reinforce disconnection from your body and emotions. Many unconsciously use meditation or excessive prayer to support dissociation from the body.

Spiritual bypassing is a withdrawal from the body and the fullness of emotions. Like other survival strategies, it only prolongs trauma's negative impact. You may feel you're growing spiritually and succeeding in your professional life, and even your relationships may seem fine, but the deep intimacy of true connection and authentic expression is not available to you. Faced with difficulties or true intimacy, you may shift into what you could call a spiritual dimension, but it's a realm disconnected from the body and emotion and from deep contact with another. You may have to pay attention in intimate or difficult situations to notice this, then journal about your experiences and reflect on your reflections, to open a deeper window into yourself to see if you are spiritualizing or intellectualizing.

Spiritual bypassing does not mean your spiritual experiences are not valid or real; quite the contrary. The depth of your practice may be profound, yet if there is significant dissociation, implicit (unconscious) trauma memories could emerge at any time to obscure your spiritual connection.

Having read this, do you sense that your spiritual practice or beliefs could be a form of spiritual bypassing? Do you use meditation or prayer—or study or work—to *not feel*? Do you tend to spiritualize, infusing difficult situations with spiritual content, avoiding the bodily experience of what may be occurring? Do you tend to need to figure things out rather than have a direct experience of maybe occurring? Write your thoughts here.

_____

_____

_____

_____

Intellectualizing

This common avoidance strategy—retreating into the intellect to avoid the body, emotions, and intimate contact with others—is another type of bypassing. It's an adaptation to frightening early life situations, a means to escape the unbearable in the body. Children who suffer profound trauma are flung out of their innate ability for embodiment and capacity to tolerate emotion; they may come to rely on rational mental capacities.

Both spiritualizing and intellectualizing may not be obvious to you, as these patterns may have been with you since you were very young, so they feel _normal_. Of course, they _are_ normal ways of responding to trauma, arising from your conclusions about your childhood world— namely _it's not safe to dwell in the body_; _it's not safe to fully feel emotions_.

THE GOAL: EMBODIMENT

Although they appear quite passive, infants, children, or adults who shut down and dissociate are expending tremendous amounts of life energy to keep unbearable feelings outside of their awareness. Intellectualizing or spiritualizing keeps a person from the inner experience of the body. Ultimately this becomes a very painful way of being.

Intellectualizing or spiritualizing can become a primary defense against what was intolerable in the interpersonal world in infancy or childhood. It can last a lifetime, preventing _embodiment_. The term _embodiment_ refers to a grounded vibrancy and feeling of being at home in your body. With trauma, parts of your experience are split off from your awareness, as it's simply too painful to experience them. Embodiment emerges as you gather, individuate, and integrate all of your parts, and you arrive, maybe for the first time, in a bodily state of wholeness and coherence. This is your trajectory of healing as you go through the workbook; we will explore it in more depth in chapter 9.

By healing trauma, you'll naturally reconnect to your body. When you address trauma somatically, you're bringing awareness to your body. Through being with your body this way you're giving yourself elements that may have been missing in the traumatic event; this is very soothing and regulating. For instance, you're attuning to your body, perhaps feeling into what your needs are in the moment, managing difficult sensations, and simultaneously learning how to stay present with them. This gives your body safety and an opportunity to reorganize at the nervous system level, which allows for a natural reconnection.

As you face inner difficulties, you're learning to see them objectively. Previously they may have obscured your ability to see clearly outside of or beyond your erroneous beliefs about yourself and the world. Your perspective widens, and the emergent potential of your human complexity is restored. You integrate the forgotten yet implicit memories of your life, replacing fragmentation and dissociation with wholeness and coherence. You emerge with a developed, more complex sense of confidence and personal agency. The split-off, traumatized parts of your consciousness are reintegrated in your body and conscious awareness. (We'll explore the split-off parts of your consciousness in later chapters.)

Your expanding perspective allows you to relate more receptively to yourself, others, and the world around you. The limitations that trauma brought on you begin to dissolve. This takes some work and courage, of course, as you're facing what once felt intolerable. That was then, and this is now. As your awareness develops and split of parts of your experience integrate, you'll recognize this more often, as you will be less likely to view the world through the lens of your traumatized past. You have many more resources, and you're no longer facing danger, even though your body and beliefs may tell you that you are.

PAUSE FOR REFLECTION: Dissolving Avoidance Patterns

The sooner you recognize your ways of avoiding feeling the pain of trauma, the easier it will become to dissolve that pattern and develop healthier ways of being. Spend some time contemplating the following questions, then notice how it feels to acknowledge any questions you answered yes to.

- Do you tend to intellectualize, retreating to your intellect or thinking
  processes when difficulties arise?   Yes   No

- Do you think about your feelings and emotions rather than feeling them?   Yes   No

- Do you retreat to spiritual beliefs, practices, or places, to avoid distress, emotions, or contact with others?   Yes   No

If you weren't sure, the next questions may help you gain insight:

- Do you feel anxious when asked to notice how your body feels?   Yes   No

- Do you find it difficult to know what's going on in your body?   Yes   No

- Do you tend to be ambivalent toward personal relationships?   Yes   No

- Do you avoid intimacy even though you may long for it?   Yes   No

- Do you tend to break contact with others in emotional or disturbing situations?   Yes   No

- Do you ever feel spiritually or intellectually superior?   Yes   No

- When you're outside of your comfortable role—business manager, teacher, mother, CEO—do you feel uncomfortable?   Yes   No

- Do you have any other insights about intellectualizing or spiritualizing your life?

  _____

  _____

  _____

  _____

- Would you rather meditate, and disconnect from what feels uncomfortable, than face a difficult situation?   Yes   No

- Do you rely on praying for help, not realizing you're bypassing your own capacity to help yourself and therefore empower yourself with a greater sense of agency?   Yes   No

How are you feeling after the exploration of dissociation and bypassing so far? It's a lot to digest. Allow yourself some time to feel your body as you have insights and assimilate what you are learning. Now let's look return to my client Frank's story to tie together a shock trauma and developmental trauma.

INTERTWINING ACUTE AND DEVELOPMENTAL TRAUMA

As a child growing up in a family where there was abuse and little relational bonding, Frank dissociated from his fearful emotions, thoughts, isolation, and loneliness. Yet after being held up at knifepoint, it seemed that all his childhood anxiety and fear resurfaced with a fury, and he could no longer keep it out of his awareness. He was tormented with a conscious daily experience of anxiety and fear until he resolved his frightening past.

As Frank experienced, shock trauma often arouses earlier developmental trauma symptoms. Let's briefly return to developmental trauma—specifically, the innate flow of defense responses. When an infant feels frightened, the first defensive response is to cry, seeking the caregiver's attention. However, very early in the infant's life, if the crying doesn't bring a comforting response, the infant can determine that crying is an unreliable or even futile strategy.[28] The next line of defense for an infant, and often for a child, is dissociation and shutting down to manage their stress.

This automatic dissociation comes when a child's distress feels intolerable. If you were distressed as an infant, you would initially go into a high state of arousal, crying and screaming, your heart pounding—a state of overwhelming panic. With continued lack of attention, you'd shift into a state of collapse, immobility, and dissociation.[29] Infants and children are powerless to discharge that high arousal energy, so they respond with physiological constriction and immobility. This pattern can last into adulthood.

The dissociated emotion and vibrant life energy are bound in your body—in your nervous system, joints, and viscera—held as physical tensions and other somatizations—physical expressions of unresolved stress and emotions. Often psychological stress manifests in physical symptoms, for which people seek medical help, not realizing their symptoms are trauma based. Because these dissociated emotions are unconscious and encoded in your body, turning toward images, imagination, the body, and its gestures—rather than using word-based interventions—can better help you resolve the effects of early trauma. These approaches promote neurological changes that boost your resilience and enable healing.

How are you feeling after reading and doing the exercises? The next exercise is an initial process to help you attune to your body, needs, and emotions through cultivating body awareness, observation, and listening. You'll explore this topic more in chapter 5.

EXERCISE: Self-Observation

For a few minutes, notice what you're experiencing, right now, in this moment. I've provided a few questions that may help you focus your awareness.

- What are you noticing in your body just now? Remember, *nothing* or *numbness* are valid answers.

  _____

- Does it feel overwhelming to feel your body—or to not feel your body? If so, try grounding, and then observe anything in your experience other than your body.

- If your body is numb, what is that like for you to notice?

  _____

- What is it like for you to notice sensations in your body, without having to do anything but simply notice? What changes do you notice as you observe sensations?

  _____

- When you bring awareness to your body, do you feel more anxious or triggered or activated? If so, use some of your resources to calm or orient yourself. Then see if you can tolerate more and observe until the sensations feel calmer.

- Is it pleasant to notice your body? If yes, how so?

  _____

- Can you notice your whole body as a field of sensations? That is more of an advanced experience, but give it a try. How is it to observe your body like this?

  _____

- Are you aware of any emotions right now? What is it like to notice?

  _____

- How would you describe your state of mind right now? Quiet, anxious, ruminating, calm?

  _____

- What else do you notice? For example, memories or images; feeling spacey, disconnected, connected, or grounded.

  Record your experiences.

  _____

  _____

  _____

GENTLY RECONNECTING

If you tend to spiritualize or intellectualize and are dissociated from your body, it's vital that you have resources to turn to as you attempt to reconnect. Prematurely reconnecting to your body can be retraumatizing, so it's important not to pressure yourself in any way as you do. Small steps are recommended. The exercises in the first part of the book were not only for your self-assessment but also a gentle guide to building resiliency and your capacity for self-regulation and connection.

A trauma-oriented therapist can provide essential support and help you work with and through the difficult emotions that reemerge as you heal. If you can't or don't want to see a therapist, I strongly recommend that you find some means of connection with another or others who can support you in your healing journey.

WHAT I LEARNED IN THIS CHAPTER

- After reading this chapter, what feels particularly relevant for you personally?

  _____

  _____

- What insights have you gained about your own traumatic responses?

  _____

  _____

- How has your understanding of the relationship between trauma and spirituality deepened?

  _____

  _____

CHAPTER 4

Activate Your Recovery System with Breathing

The flow of breath in your body offers a healing and life-giving presence. Breath is the primordial foundation of the human spirit. Your breath carries oxygen into your body and your voice into the world. Research has demonstrated that conscious breathing is an important component of healing trauma. And just as ancient mariners learned to navigate the sea's unpredictable currents and storms by working with the wind, you can learn to use your breath to navigate trauma's inner storms and currents.

Conscious breathing is a key for healing and energizing your body and mind. The depth of your breath should be enough to invigorate and enliven you. Too much breath, and you become lightheaded; too little, and you become sluggish and dull. Yogis believe that specific breathing techniques infuse the body with *prana*—life force. Certain breathing techniques can deepen self-awareness and self-knowledge as they allow your life force to flow more freely, clearing blockages that obscure your essential nature. The breathing techniques in this chapter will also help you restore balance to your psychobiology.

Many breathing techniques are used in mental health treatment modalities for stress- and trauma-related disorders. These techniques have shown potential to resolve long-term symptoms of trauma.[30] Through consciously guiding your breath, you'll feel an increased sense of vitality and aliveness. As you build your breathing practice, you can recalibrate your whole system—body, mind, and spirit—to enhance healing.

You can use your breath to:

- Find calm when you feel upset, triggered, or unsettled

- Bring yourself out of shutdown states and patterns of isolation and withdrawal

- Reconnect and center yourself in the moment, bringing a welcome space between now and the past

- Be present to what you're feeling without clenching your jaw, frowning, becoming defensive, isolating, or freezing

- Enhance your capacity to self-regulate, allowing you to gain clarity and insight into situations that may be or have been troubling

If you're experiencing fears that seem to have no origin in the moment but may limit your engagement in and enjoyment of life, being in the flow of conscious breathing helps you be right here, right now, with less or no fear. Having less fear shifts you from a sense of separateness to unity.

THE MOVEMENT OF YOUR BREATH

You're going to explore your breath from a variety of perspectives—physiological, Eastern yogic, and experiential—through powerful exercises proven to enhance PTG. For now, bring your awareness to your breath and take an inventory of your breathing pattern. In the next exercise, I offer some examples of patterns you may notice. You may have more than one breathing pattern; it may change depending on the situation. It may even change as you observe it in the moment. This exercise is for your initial self-assessment; use what you observe as a reference point for seeing how your breathing patterns may improve during your healing journey.

EXERCISE: How Do You Breathe?

Bring your awareness to your body and your breath and simply notice how you breathe. Underline the patterns that apply to you and describe any additional things you observe.

- My breath is shallow.

- My breath feels smooth.

- My breath feels jarring.

- I breathe only into my upper chest.

- I barely feel the movement of my breath.

- I breathe into my belly and my chest.

- I tend to hold my breath when I inhale.

- I tend to not fully exhale.

- I tend to hold my breath after breathing out and hesitate on the inhalation.

- I feel uncomfortable when I pay attention to my breath.

- Observing my breath brings a sense of calm.

- _____

- _____

- _____

Once you become familiar and comfortable with noticing your breath and can simply follow its movement, thinking begins to ease, internal chatter gradually slows, words begin to dissolve with each exhalation. Breath has a certain timelessness. Befriending the breath allows you to gently come to your body and into the moment.

When practicing observing your breath, seek an environment that nourishes you: perhaps in nature, where you can embrace aesthetics both inwardly and outwardly, or a quiet space filled with a scent that relaxes you or colors and fabrics that exude peacefulness. Find your creative elements of nurturance as you become more present with yourself for more soothing support and a deepening sense of safety.

For successful practice of any breath exercise, sit in a way that makes it easy to breathe. As much as you can, sit comfortably so your spine is upright and aligned, with your chin slightly tucked to lengthen the back of your neck—this posture allows you to feel more connected to your body. Slouching creates a subtle dullness of mind; your awareness is more likely to wander off into your thoughts and away from your breath. Using more muscle energy, as you do in this upright posture, improves your awareness and helps keep your mind alert.

Read through the instructions before you do this next exercise. They're easy to remember, and this will help you get the most benefit.

EXERCISE: Observing Your Breath

1. For a couple of minutes, simply observe your breath.

2. Pay attention to the inhale. How deeply does it move into your body?

3. Now, observe the exhale. Is it complete or partial?

4. See if you can notice the point at which your breath moves from the inhale to the exhale.

5. As you follow the inhale and exhale, notice where you feel the breath—your nose, chest, or belly. Once you've practiced this for a few minutes, continue with the next section.

6. Choose one place in your body where you notice the breath and focus your awareness there.

7. Now anchor your awareness in this place and simply be with the movement and the sensations you feel there. Keep this very simple. If your mind wanders, simply bring your awareness back to your body and your breath.

How was this practice for you?

_____

_____

_____

_____

Were you able to notice the point where your inhalation and exhalation met? What did that point feel like?

_____

Was it easy or challenging for you to stay focused, observing and feeling your breath? What made it easy or challenging?

_____

_____

_____

When you noticed your mind wandering, were you able to return your awareness to your breath? Did any sensations accompany that return?

_____

_____

_____

If your mind did wander, how was it to return your awareness to your breath? Was this way pleasant, unpleasant, or neutral?

_____

_____

DEVELOPING YOUR BREATHING PRACTICE

A word of caution before you start the more complex breathing exercises that follow. Breathwork is powerful and can be very transformative. It's not only your physical breath, but the energetic nature of your breath that resonates deeply through your body. These breathing practices can neutralize your psychological defenses, allowing unconscious material such as forgotten memories and frozen emotions to surface. They can free your life force that was stuck in fight, flight, or freeze responses in your body. It's very important to monitor any changes in all aspects of your experience as you do these exercises. Slow down when you need to. Some simple guidelines:

- As you begin each exercise, see if you can locate and feel some level of safety.

- Maintain a level of safety as you continue.

- Check in with yourself often to make sure you're grounded.

- Notice if you're in contact with your body. If you dissociate or feel disconnected or unsafe, stop that exercise and use any of the exercises from previous chapters that helped you reconnect and feel safe and centered. You can return to the breathing exercise once you're feeling safe again.

You're building a wonderful repertoire of self-regulating and emotional regulating practices. With each breath in the following exercises you're renewing and restoring the relationship between your body, mind and spirit. Stay aware of and monitor your experience. A slow and steady approach will yield the best results most quickly.

PRANA, BREATH, AND SUBTLE ENERGY

Your breath is closely connected with the subtle energy called prana in the yogic tradition and chi in Chinese medicine; I refer to it as life force. Your breath is a tangible bridge between subtle energy and your body. The principles of subtle energy and subtle physiology are found in several doctrines in Eastern culture, including the yogic and tantric systems, Buddhist psychology, Chinese and Japanese esotericism, and the mystical traditions of Christianity, Judaism, and Islam, as well as in various traditions of martial arts.

The ancient Eastern traditions hold that our physical body rests within the subtle body, and the subtle body permeates the physical. These traditions suggest that you can direct the flow of subtle energy within the physical to attain higher states of consciousness and greater health and overall well-being. These principles are seen in the practice of yoga, tai chi, and qigong, in which, along with movement, the breath is also used for the exchange of energy between the subtle and the physical body. As you'll read later in this chapter, neuroscience has now validated the efficaciousness of the powerful breathing techniques that have long been used in the East.

A basic understanding is ample for you to experience healing and to help transform the difficulties that arise from trauma. As you practice the exercises in this chapter, you may experience for yourself the relationship between your physical and subtle body.

The following breathing exercises are drawn from the Eastern yogic tradition and are known as *pranayama*, a Sanskrit term meaning control of breath. Your breath is the source of prana, and in controlling your breath in these exercises you'll influence your well-being, state of mind, and sense of spirituality.

ALTERNATE NOSTRIL BREATHING AND THE SUBTLE ENERGY CHANNELS

This exercise has been shown to produce the following benefits:

- Relaxes the body and mind

- Helps reduce insomnia

- Soothes racing thoughts

- Calms anxiety

- Sharpens mental clarity and capacity for concentration

- Clears subtle energy channels

Nadi is the term for energy channel in traditional Indian medicine (similar to the meridians in the Chinese medicine system). In yoga philosophy, the concept of the nadis has about three thousand years of history. It's through the nadis, of which you have many thousands, that the subtle energies flow through your physical body.

To heal trauma using the practice of alternate nostril breathing, you're directly influencing two specific nadis—*ida* and *pingala*—that begin at your low back and run alongside your spine. Ida nadi, the left side, terminates at the left nostril. Pingala nadi, the right side, terminates at the right nostril. As you breathe through each nostril, the subtle energetic channels are said to be cleared, which enhances the circulation of prana within you.

As with all the exercises, first read the directions all the way through before you begin. (An audio recording of instructions for this exercise is available at http://www.newharbinger .com/43256.)

EXERCISE: Nadi Shodhana Pranayama to Enhance Life Force

1. Seat yourself comfortably, with a pillow on your lap to rest your elbow on.

2. Make the hand gesture by curling your right pinky finger over the ring finger. Curl your index and middle finger into your palm or point them upward, resting between your eyebrows.

3. Now rest the thumb and ring finger of your right hand on the side of each nostril; don't press your nostril closed yet. If you can't get your hand into this position, use your index finger and thumb instead.

4. Inhale a basic, full belly breath, letting your diaphragm drop and your belly expand as fully as possible.

5. Exhale through both nostrils. As you exhale, allow your belly to hollow out as you intentionally pull it in and back toward the spine.

6. Keeping your belly relaxed, use your thumb to close your *right* nostril as you inhale slowly and fully through the *left*.

7. Hold for a moment, then release your thumb from your *right* nostril and cover your *left* nostril with your ring or index finger as you exhale slowly through your *right* nostril.

8. Inhale through your right nostril. Hold for a moment.

9. Now cover your right nostril. Release the left and exhale through it.

This completes one round of alternate nostril breathing. In each round, you inhale through one nostril and exhale through the other, inhale through the nostril you just exhaled through and exhale out the other.

1. Practice this for 5 to 10 rounds if you can, then take a short break. If you feel okay, do a few more rounds.

2. Record your experience with this practice in the space provided. Note how many rounds you're comfortable with. Over time you'll be able to do more rounds at one time, developing a longer practice.

_____

_____

_____

_____

Alternate nostril pranayama is very calming. Occasionally people feel anxious when practicing this breath. If you do, simply skip it and try the next exercises. This practice can be done at any time; try it at bedtime.

VICTORIOUS BREATH

Before we explore how breathing techniques work to heal trauma, viewed from a Western medical perspective, you'll learn another breathing exercise. Ujjayi breath, also known as victorious breath, is known to be both energizing and calming because of its balancing influence on the cardiovascular system. Here are a few of its benefits:

- Calms anxiety

- Helps reduce stress, insomnia, and symptoms of depression

- Regulates blood pressure

- Helps enhance mental alertness

- Stimulates the vagus nerve enhancing PNS vagal tone (explained later in the chapter)

- Encourages the flow of vital life force

With ujjayi breath, you gently constrict your airway in the back of your throat by contracting the laryngeal muscles and partially closing the glottis. As the breath moves, you make a hissing sound that has been described as waves on the ocean, Darth Vader's breathing, or the sound a scuba diver makes! When you feel irritated, nervous, or agitated, the rhythmic nature of the ujjayi breath is very calming to your entire nervous system. (An audio recording of instructions for this exercise is available at http://www.newharbinger.com/43256.)

EXERCISE: Ujjayi Breathing for Inner Balance

1. With your mouth closed, breathe in and out through your nose. Continue to breathe through your nose (not through your mouth) for the entire practice.

2. Take a deep inhalation.

3. As you *slowly* exhale, constrict the muscles in the back of your throat and make the hissing sound. This may take some practice to find the right amount of constriction and the hissing sound.

4. As you inhale, fill your belly first, then your lower rib cage, then upper.

5. On the exhale, empty your upper chest, then your lower rib cage, and then your belly. Keep the length of the inhalation and the exhalation the same.

6. After five to ten minutes of practice, record your experience of Ujjayi breathing.

_____

_____

_____

Right after doing a breathing exercise, you may notice quiet moments; these can serve as ground for spontaneous creative images or inner silence, which can help with integration and body coherence. Simply remain in the quiet.

Now let's look at the healthy physiological effects of your breathing practice, and how it affects your heart rate and overall well-being.

HEART RATE VARIABILITY AND YOUR BREATH

You may think your heart beats with a steady rhythm; however, the time between beats varies depending on a variety of changing conditions.[31] This variability in the time interval between successive heartbeats is called *heart rate variability* (HRV). A healthy heartbeat has irregularities. If the intervals between heartbeats is too constant, that is considered low HRV. If the length varies, HRV is said to be high. Understanding HRV could help your healing process, as HRV measures how much your heart rate corresponds to your breathing.

High HRV is associated with better health and longevity. Low HRV is associated with chronic stress, anxiety, panic, PTSD, depression, and aging. Research indicates that epigenetic factors can also influence a person's tendency toward high or low HRV.[32] Keep in mind that HRV is one of many factors that represent and contribute to your overall health.

Ongoing unresolved trauma is thought to create poor or reduced HRV. With low HRV you may either under- or overreact to stress. When you perceive danger or a life threat, your HRV goes down; when you perceive safety, it goes up. If your HRV is low due to trauma, heightening it can create more efficient regulation of emotion and your overall well-being. Ultimately, your HRV reflects your capacity to meet changing situations—the degree of modulation of your cardiac activity and your capacity to regulate your emotional expression and your cognitive and social levels of well-being and health.

Breathing techniques are especially effective in improving HRV that's low due to adversity and stress.[33] Slow breathing techniques, like alternate nostril breathing and ujjayi breath, are also a wonderful way to reduce overactivity in your amygdala (which I'll discuss in chapter 7) and boost activity in the emotional regulatory centers of your prefrontal cortex, contributing to greater mental clarity.[34]

VAGUS NERVE, VAGAL TONE, AND YOUR ABILITY TO ADAPT

You can improve HRV by working with the vagus nerve and its activity: *vagal tone*. Vagus nerve impulses inhibit heartbeat to keep the heart beating within a safe range, so vagal tone is a marker of emotional regulation, emotional reactivity, and expression, indicating how well you can psychologically adapt to different conditions.[35]

There are two branches of the vagus nerve: (1) the dorsal branch, involved in immobilization behaviors, and (2) the ventral branch, involved in social and calming behavior—think face-to-face contact, and feelings of safety. Both influence the heart and vagal tone. Again, increased vagal tone is associated with greater HRV. You can enhance your vagal tone with the specific breathing techniques in this chapter.

Many of the neural pathways of the PNS are connected to the vagus nerve. The motor fibers in the vagus nerve provide the brain with continuous information about the status of your organs including your heart and gut. Stimulating the vagus nerve through yogic breathing techniques calms your brain, heart, and gut—your digestive track and gastrointestinal sensitivity.[36] The amicable mind-body practice of conscious breathing exercises the neural pathways directly connected to the vagus circuits, promoting neurophysiological states that support your health and well-being.[37]

BELLOWS BREATH

Bellows breath is a rapid, forceful breathing technique that can increase your alertness, energy, and attention. It is typically practiced for only a few minutes at a time. I recommend that you initially practice it for only a few breaths. Bellows breath helps you begin to feel increased energy while being still, bringing feelings of excitation followed by calmness. Observe how this feels in your body. It provides a gentle sympathetic stimulation similar to regular physical exercise and increases your sympathetic nervous system's ability to respond to stress without fatigue. This energizing breath is great to practice in the morning or when you feel lethargic, sleepy, withdrawn, or shut down. (An audio recording of instructions for this exercise is available at http://www.newharbinger.com/43256.)

A cautionary note: If you suffer severe PTSD, flashbacks, or any respiratory condition, don't practice this technique without a teacher present. Don't practice it if you're pregnant or have hypertension, epilepsy, or seizures. Because you're going to be contracting your belly, wait at least two hours after eating before you practice. Lightheadedness is quite common at first. If that happens, pause and breathe normally; when the discomfort passes, try another round, with a little less intensity. After you finish, observe your body's response.

EXERCISE: Bellows Breath for Resilience

1. Sit in your best upright posture while relaxing your body. Inhale and exhale through your nose a few times.

2. Exhale forcefully through your nose while pulling your belly in toward your spine. At the end of the exhale, relax.

3. Allow yourself to inhale naturally and without effort.

4. Exhale forcefully again, forcing the air out of your nostrils while pulling in your belly.

5. Allow yourself to inhale naturally.

6. Repeat this pattern of breathing four or five times, then pause. As you become more familiar with the technique you can do more.

These breathing exercises will help you expand your tolerance for what feels uncomfortable or intolerable. Before long, as you combine the breath work with the other exercises, you'll be able to stay present to what once felt overwhelming and fearful. As you increase your ability to tolerate the difficult and painful parts of your experience, you're also expanding your capacity to feel pleasant experiences. A courageous dance occurs at the edge of your tolerance as you take small, gradual, tolerable risks. Little by little your body—the vessel of your life force, sensation, thought, and emotion—can hold and tolerate more.

FEAR OF THE UNFAMILIAR

Caution: Breathwork can bring a state of coherence and stability that feels very quiet and calm in your body/mind system. Although this may sound desirable, it may also be unnerving. It can feel unfamiliar, which can be scary. When you live with trauma, whether it's developmental or shock trauma, unaccustomed feelings and sensations can be like an amygdala alert. Even though you're safe and okay, it can seem like the quiet before a looming storm. If these breathing exercises evoke any fear, remember the helpful tools you've learned. You already know much more about trauma and have developed ways to cope and heal. This can help you recognize and normalize your experiences.

HOW BREATHING EXERCISES CAN CHANGE YOUR MIND

These breathing techniques are known to balance and improve ANS functioning and help regulate it, a major key to healing trauma. This improvement of ANS functioning is a result of *enhancing* the activation of parasympathetic functioning when you feel shut down or withdrawn or lethargic and by *lessening* sympathetic arousal when you feel *too much*.

Research has identified additional benefits of these breathing techniques:

- Balancing your brain's left and right hemispheres

- Allowing unconscious material to come into your awareness, which supports healing (for trauma, this may include painful emotions and repressed memories)

- Facilitating physical and mental calmness

- Building SNS stability so you can respond to stress without becoming fatigued or overwhelmed

- Helping alleviate anxiety, insomnia, and depression

- Deeply relaxing body and mind, while calming racing thoughts

- Enhancing a sense of spiritual connection

- Enabling your body to contain higher charges of energy, arousal, and emotion without feeling overwhelmed

- Possibly alleviating and helping you manage physical pain

Researchers have identified neural connections between the brain's respiratory control center and the center controlling state of mind. Researchers from Stanford University School of Medicine identified a small cluster of neurons that link breathing patterns to relaxation, attention, excitement, and anxiety. Their discoveries show how breath-control exercises can relieve stress disorders and help you achieve a meditative wakeful state—calm, present, and mentally alert. The meditative state produced through breathing exercises tends to be safe for people with unresolved trauma. It naturally supports being more embodied and less dissociated. So if you're drawn to spiritual practices, using the breath in meditation or movement can enhance your practice as it keeps you connected to your body.

CONCLUDING THOUGHTS

The literature on therapeutic breathing techniques for stress- and trauma-related symptoms continues to expand, and these simple practices offer many other health benefits. Although they may initially feel awkward, once you become more familiar with them through practice, you may begin to really enjoy your breathwork time. As you learn and develop your practice, it's ideal to find a trained pranayama teacher (ask at your local yoga studio). With a teacher or on your own, if you follow these basic instructions and practice slowly and mindfully, these simple breathing exercises are gentle, yet powerful enough to create positive shifts in your physiology and subtle energy systems.

WHAT I LEARNED IN THIS CHAPTER

Spend some time reflecting on the breathing techniques that you learned and how they have helped you overall. Describe your relationship to subtle energy now and the feelings of aliveness within you. Describe how it feels to use your breath for calming or invigoration, depending on what you need.

_____

_____

_____

_____

_____

_____

CHAPTER 5

Let Your Innate Qualities Shine

A profound expression of gratitude welled up from one of my clients, whose tumultuous life left her feeling far removed from any form of thankfulness. Bent over in sadness and intense shame, she noticed the shiny black patent leather of her shoes. "My shoes," she said, slowly sitting upright. "I'm grateful for my shoes."

The unfurling of her body, and her tears of joy at finding something real that she was thankful for, opened her to hope and a glimmer of aliveness. Sitting upright, she repeatedly expressed her gratitude for having shoes. She breathed deeper, felt a softening in her chest, and recognized many other things for which she was grateful—the small bonsai tree she cared for in her kitchen, her ability to come to therapy, the stray cat she had taken in that gave her company and a sense of connection.

Trauma can blind you to what is good in your life. Gratitude slowly opens the heart to recognize the beauty of what you do have, and it can begin with the simplest of things. With continued practice, your gratitude can grow.

Gratitude is a very simple practice, and one of the easiest ways to shift the brain toward positive emotions and away from stress, anxiety, depression, and loneliness.[38] Gratitude has been shown to improve sleep and increase resilience and optimism in the long run.[39] Including gratitude in a daily practice regimen will help you expand your tolerance for what feels stressful or was once so uncomfortable you had to disconnect. Your overall psychological health will improve with gratitude.

Unresolved anger often presents as wanting to hurt others for the pain you feel or felt, or the damage done. It can hold you captive, as revenge seems easier than feeling the sorrow and grief of what was lost in the trauma. Something is always lost—connection, trust, your capacity to feel, your authentic expression—yet something can also be gained. Gratitude reduces aggression, increases empathy toward others, and diminishes the desire for revenge. These very unpleasant longings for revenge can be remedied and transformed as you integrate your emotions. Not everyone experiences a hunger for retaliation, of course; for some people it's a feeling they had to split off when they were a child, and because that feeling was not integrated, it still affects them to some degree. As you practice gratitude, you'll experience lower negative effects of toxic emotions, including unintegrated anger, resentment, frustration, and regret.

The following exercises have a wonderful positive influence on your well-being.

EXERCISE: Cultivating Gratitude

Spend a few moments contemplating what you're grateful for and record it here.

I'm grateful for:

_____

_____

_____

Practice of Gratitude

1. Sit in an upright posture, feeling the length of your spine. Consciously soften the front of your body and feel the strength of the back of your body.

2. Bring your attention to the center of your chest—your heart center—and say quietly or out loud five things you're grateful for: "I'm grateful for …" Then pause for a few seconds.

3. Repeat the exercise; it may be the same five things each time or others that spontaneously occur to you.

4. Pause and simply notice any subtle change you feel in your body, breath, or mind.

5. Record any changes you noticed in your body and your whole experience.

_____

_____

_____

Cultivating gratitude is a good evening or morning practice. Of course, you can practice this as much as you like throughout the day.

SPIRITUAL PRACTICE ENHANCES POST-TRAUMATIC GROWTH

When traumatic symptoms are affecting your life, research has shown that if you include the development of a spiritual practice—such as cultivating gratitude, loving kindness, and compassion—in your healing process, you're more likely to achieve a positive outcome. A spiritual practice will not only help you heal from trauma but also help you sustain your sense of well-being over time. While your initial motivation for developing a spiritual practice may be healing from trauma, the benefits may go far beyond freeing yourself from trauma's debilitating effects. Or you may already have a spiritual practice and may be adding the more embodied practices or practicing other exercises to support you in the embodiment process.

Remember: what fosters growth is not the trauma itself, but the process of coping with and resolving it. People experiencing PTG often encounter what feels like a "second chance" at life. Including spirituality in your approach to healing trauma, especially if you develop and continue with a spiritual practice, favors such a second chance.

STAYING WITH NEGATIVE AND POSITIVE EMOTIONS THROUGH LOVING KINDNESS

In your healing journey, you must learn to tolerate both negative and positive emotions. Emotions in themselves are not good or bad. They're but a variety of human expressions. If you want to increase your capacity for resilience, joy, and love, and have as full a life as possible, being able to tolerate a wide range of emotions is essential.

Again, healing is not linear. It's often discontinuous and labyrinthine. In recovering from trauma, your brain moves from organization to disorganization and back to organization, each time establishing *higher levels* of organization.

In the disorganization phase, your old trauma patterns destabilize. It's then vital to develop the capacity to tolerate and stay with any discomfort, fear, or negative emotion that arises, without your typical reactivity. As you stay aware of your body, sensations and emotions, observing yourself in the present, your brain shifts into a state of organization at a *higher level*.

Gradually your habitual patterns of defensiveness, reactivity, disconnection, and dissociation are mitigated. You're rewiring your brain, cultivating calmer ways of being.

You can cultivate loving kindness and compassion using two practices drawn from the Buddhist tradition. They are part of the four immeasurables or divine abodes, translated from the Sanskrit *brahmavihāra*. They open your heart center, counter distortions or unpleasant feelings you may have about yourself, and deepen your relationship with yourself and others.

Loving kindness opens you to love that you may be blocking. Loving kindness is directly related to releasing your fear about love or, more directly, of not being loved or of losing love. If you experienced the fear of losing your loving relationship to your parents when young, or a devastating heartbreak as an adolescent or adult, love can become frightening; the potential pain can seem too much to bear. In response, you block yourself from both giving and receiving love. It can be tricky to recognize this!

Heartbreak registers in the body like a trauma. Bring your broken heart—whether from a traumatic event or the loss of love or feelings of being unloved—to a quiet space, and allow the sting of your wounding to be bathed in these healing practices.

EXERCISE: Loving Kindness

1. Find the meditative posture you used for the breathing practices. Bring your attention to your heart center and repeat these statements aloud, with focus, for a few minutes, then repeat silently for a few minutes.

    -   May I be filled with loving kindness.

    -   May I be filled with peace.

    -   May I find inner joy.

2. Was this practice easy for you or challenging? Record any struggles that came up.

    _____

    _____

3. Were you able to stay with the phrases for a few minutes?   **Yes   No**

4. What changes did you notice in your body?

_____

_____

5. Did you notice any changes in your overall mood or emotional state? Write down how you feel emotionally now, after doing the practice.

_____

_____

_____

You can do these simple yet powerful practices anytime, but it becomes more powerful when you sit with focused intention and _feel_ the words. See if you can build up to a period of ten to twenty minutes as you repeat the words, then give yourself a few minutes to simply sit in silence to feel the effects of your practice.

If your heart seems so inclined, radiate loving kindness out to those around you in ever-widening circles. Simply change "May I" to "May we." The positive benefits of a practice of loving kindness include greater social connection.

SURRENDERING TO YOUR NEED FOR LOVE AND CONNECTION

In wishing to experience loving kindness, you're conveying a gesture of vulnerability, a surrender to the deep human need for love and connection. The risk we take in loving is to be denied being loved. For many of us, this is a long-held unconscious fear. For a child, losing love feels unbearable; it seems easier to close off from love than to ever have to face that unbearable pain again. Yet if you've closed off from love in any form, as you practice you may experience a deep sadness or grief. Your emotions give a depth of meaning to what is happening, so allow them to well up, as much as you're able. It is paradoxically very painful to begin to receive what you may once have been denied; the pain will diminish as you practice.

When you practice loving kindness, you create just that. You'll no longer feel dependent on others' love for your survival, as love becomes more of who you find yourself to be. Seen this way, cultivating loving kindness for yourself isn't a reification of a lone, separate self, but a metamorphosis of a contracted heart into one full of beauty and interconnected with others. This is not a transactional beauty but a reflection of your consciousness. When you don't fear love, it's more likely to show up in your life. As Rumi expressed so beautifully, "Your task is not to 'seek' for Love—but merely to seek and find all the 'barriers' within yourself, that you've built against Love." This is at the heart of the resolution of trauma and the essence of this workbook.

UNDERSTANDING COMPASSION

The book the *Monastery and the Microscope* includes a favorite story from Richard Davidson, a professor of psychology and psychiatry at the University of Wisconsin.[40] Davidson, neuroscientist Francisco Varela, and other scientists were explaining to over two hundred monks at Namgyal Monastery how brain activity was recorded. Electrodes were placed on Francisco's head. As the technicians moved out of the way, revealing Francisco with all the wires attached to his head, the monks burst out laughing. They found the idea of studying compassion from the head rather than the heart hilarious.

There is an immediate and strong connection between your heart and areas of your brain. From a scientific viewpoint, every experience has a correlate in the brain. This knowledge can help us understand what practices are helpful in healing trauma. But your subjective experience is most important. In the practice of loving kindness and the upcoming compassion exercise, you may experience a feeling of warmth, or a gentle softening somewhere in your body, or intrusive thoughts may begin to loosen their grip. Feel into this, your own positive subjective experience.

How Empathy Relates to Compassion

In their book *Altered Traits*, psychologists and researchers Daniel Goleman and Richard Davidson wrote about three types of empathy.[41] One is *cognitive empathy*, which allows you to see another's perspective and understand how they think. With *emotional empathy*, you can feel what another is feeling. This can be disturbing, as feeling another's distress may light up your own brain's distress signals, causing you to want to avoid them. This is understandable, especially if you're already feeling distress. Then there is *empathic caring*, which is related to compassion. This form of empathy creates positive feelings and boosts your capacity for altruism. The neural circuits that light up in your brain with compassion are like that of parental love for a child, so compassion circumvents distress,[42] engendering loving feelings. Compassion helps you accept what is happening without turning away from the pain. Thus practicing compassion cultivates courage, acceptance, and inner feelings of expansion and spaciousness.

When using the practice of compassion in trauma recovery, you must first cultivate compassion for your own being. Then compassion will begin to naturally flow beyond your previously defined boundaries. Professor of psychiatry Daniel Seigel expressed the experience beyond your defined self: "underneath our thoughts and feelings, prejudices and beliefs, there rests a grounded self that is part of a larger whole."[43]

EXERCISE: Self-Reflection: Compassion and Empathy

1. Are you an empathetic person? Describe your relationship with empathy. Do you think it helps or hinders you?

    _____

    _____

2. Are you a cognitive empath, able to see another person's perspective and how they think? Write down an example from your life.

    _____

    _____

3. Are you emotionally empathic, able to feel what another is feeling? Describe how you do or don't experience this. If you do, do you also feel distress when you feel another's distress? Record how you experience this.

    _____

    _____

    _____

4. Do you feel you're a compassionate person? Describe how this shows up in your life.

_____

_____

_____

The Benefits of Compassion

The practice of compassion is so simple, and the benefits so rich and nurturing. Research shows that a practice of compassion increases the activation of the brain circuits connected to attention, perspective taking, positive feeling, and a greater capacity for altruism.[44] Compassion will also help you develop greater resilience in the reactivation and functioning of your amygdala.[45] The amygdala is responsible for autonomic responses associated with fear and your fear conditioning. It acts like a radar, alerting your brain when it perceives something significant.

Developing these capacities is fundamental to healing trauma. The three practices of gratitude, loving kindness, and compassion internally generate qualities of mind that beg to be shared. They will enhance your natural desire and need for interconnectivity.

The following exercise is closely linked to loving kindness; it's designed to evoke a genuine sense of compassion toward yourself and your suffering. It's a wonderful antidote to self-loathing, low self-esteem, and lack of self-worth. Compassion is also a safeguard in emotional empathy, sparing you distress if you're an emotional empath.[46] With compassion, different circuits light up in your brain; the feeling tone is very different, as you'll experience in your practice. A compassionate response to suffering involves caring and a recognition of suffering's universal nature. The source of all our suffering is the same—disconnection.

EXERCISE: Cultivating Compassion

Just as in your loving kindness practice, you'll be repeating short phrases. These are best practiced and cited in a meditative posture, so sit upright, being as majestic as you can. A strong, still, and noble body is conducive for cultivating the depth of what you're asking for.

- May my pain and trauma show me the way to compassion.

- May I have compassion for my difficulties and for what happened to me.

- May I receive others' love and compassion.

- May I be free from the root of trauma.

Describe your experience of the practice:

_____

_____

_____

Record any differences you experienced between this exercise and the loving kindness exercise. Did you learn anything new about yourself?

_____

_____

_____

MOTIVATION FOR YOUR PRACTICE

Reiterating the benefits of gratitude, loving kindness, and compassion practices may motivate you to practice, as they:

- Cultivate an inner feeling of goodness and pleasantness

- Enhance your capacity for self and emotional regulation

- Increase your physical and psychological well-being

- Shift your brain toward positive emotions

- Cultivate compassion and loving kindness

- Encourage PTG and your ability to become psychologically healthier and happier than you were prior to any trauma

ATTENDING TO YOUR POSTURE

Your body is often shaped by trauma, so body awareness is vital for healing. The following exercise is designed to increase your body and posture awareness. You can shift out of slumped or contracted postures, open your body up to more feeling, and allow your life force to flow more easily by:

- Bringing awareness to your body and posture

- Rolling your shoulders back and down (helping open your chest and heart)

- Slightly tilting your pelvis to lengthen your spine

- Tucking your chin slightly, lengthening the back of your neck

All this enhances your healing exercises. Note, however, that attending to your posture can also invite in blocked emotions such as sadness or grief. If this happens and you feel too much, return to your orienting, grounding, or resourcing exercises. Or imagine the opposite:

- If the feeling of sadness or the constriction that you notice in your body doesn't lessen or worsens with attention, imagine the opposite sensation or emotion. If sadness feels like a black lump in your throat, or anger like a Tasmanian devil in your belly, imagine a bright sphere of light or a field of golden flowers, expressing joy.

- The opposite feeling you imagine could present as a color, sensation, image, or feeling. Keep imagining until your sensations and emotions change to something pleasant or less challenging.

EXERCISE: Describing your Posture

Circle any description that applies to you, and/or add your own observations at the end:

- My shoulders are slumped forward.

- My chest looks a bit collapsed.

- My spine is rounded.

- I have scoliosis.

- My head juts forward.

- My chin is always up, constricting the back of my neck.

- My shoulders are tense, hunching up toward my ears.

- My shoulders seem to be protecting my heart; my muscles look flaccid.

- Some muscles look flaccid; others are very tense and tight.

- _____

- _____

- _____

As you purposefully sit with better posture, if you notice an emotional response, ask yourself:

- Is it okay to feel sadness (or whatever emotion is present)?   **Yes   No**

- Where do I notice the sadness in my body?

  _____

- What happens if I'm curious about the sadness rather than trying to avoid it?

  _____

- What happens to my breath as I'm curious about the sadness?

  _____

- Does my body collapse in some way, or can I remain in an upright posture as I feel?

  _____

CONCLUDING THOUGHTS

You've learned how trauma creates disconnection—disconnection from yourself, your being, others, and the world around you—and the importance of reconnection. You've identified symptoms of trauma and how trauma lives in your body; that your present responses and symptoms may relate to your past; that early in your life, if your environment didn't nourish you in the way you needed, you developed adaptations, patterns, and erroneous beliefs and feelings about yourself that still distort your perception, life, and life force. By being more informed about your body/brain trauma responses and learning many helpful techniques to release trauma from your body, you're creating new life-enhancing neuronal pathways—changing your brain in healing ways.

These exercises can become lifelong practices, a way to continue enhancing your well-being, support your personal growth, and expand your consciousness. As the exercises become familiar, use them any time you feel the need. As you continue through this workbook, they will continue to help in your recovery—a strong, stable foundation on which your potential can be realized.

Enjoy the fruits of the next level of practices, which will awaken your inherent capacity for wisdom and joy.

CHAPTER 6

Embody and Integrate
Your Emotions

I've noted that you're on a journey of discovering your heart's desire—the essence of your authentic self and your unique expression of it. Developmental trauma robs you of this deep desire. Trauma obscures your capacity for authentic expression, but trauma can also be a portal to a deeper spiritual reality.

This obscuring of your true desire tends to occur in early life to maintain the attachment to and love with your caregivers. In this sacrifice on the altar of survival, there can be varying degrees of numbing, splitting, and dissociation. Those lost parts of your consciousness remain arrested in their psychospiritual growth and maturity, frozen in time. Your adaptations, defenses, and distortions of your self-perception create a false sense of self, which compensates for the loss. You identify with this false self; you come to believe it's who you are. Your authentic self is never destroyed, just concealed by a web of defenses.

This chapter begins the exploration of returning to your heart's desire by understanding and transforming barriers to your authentic expression and capacity to know you are love. With trauma, your heart closes in a protective response. It becomes very difficult to make choices that support your authentic being. This may not be obvious to you, as this closure can begin very early in life. So we begin by exploring your emotions and your relationship to them; how you can work with them rather than against them to free your heart and help you heal from trauma.

A WHOLE SPECTRUM OF BOUNTIFUL EMOTIONS

As you heal and grow, you're learning to become more comfortable with a range of states as you elicit more positive states. The absence of negative states—shame, self-doubt, fear, low self-esteem—doesn't necessarily result in a positive state, so it's important to cultivate positive states.[47]

As you're able to cultivate positive states and feelings, you'll experience greater self-esteem and presence in previously challenging or overwhelming situations. As your strong and confident sense of agency evolves, it's vital to have associated healthy self-esteem and positive emotions.[48]

Emotional stress is a proven major cause of illness. The body/brain systems that process your emotions are directly connected to those that govern health: your immune, hormonal, and nervous systems. Cultivating your ability to feel and regulate your emotions will inspire a new sense of self-reliance, confidence, *and* overall well-being. As you experience a deeper range of emotions, you restore your heart's capacity and openness to love. As your defenses soften, you can realize your heart's deepest desire.

CONSIDERING YOUR EMOTIONS

What kind of relationship do you have with your emotions? Underline the statements that ring true for you.

- I welcome my emotions.

- I experience a wide range of emotions.

- My emotional expression is limited.

- I don't like emotions.

- I'm rarely emotional.

- I notice fear when I feel some emotions.

- I struggle to identify what emotions I'm feeling.

- I feel overwhelmed by my emotions.

- Depending on the situation, I may feel emotion or I may feel numb.

The emotions I'm comfortable with are _____

_____

I'm comfortable with these emotions because _____

_____

The emotions I don't like or that feel uncomfortable are _____

_____

What I don't like about this/these emotions is _____

_____

Describe what it was like for you to acknowledge your relationship to emotions:

_____

_____

Being human means experiencing a range of emotions and emotional tones each day. For people who have experienced trauma, being able to fully feel emotions when they arise without feeling overwhelmed is an important indicator of healing. Being able to tolerate emotions and be present to them creates a positive shift both physically and psychologically, bringing a deep acceptance and appreciation of yourself and others on this amazing human journey.

Both developmental trauma and acute or shock trauma bring a cacophony of profoundly overwhelming emotions typically too intense to absorb. They can feel threatening to your very existence. After trauma, emotion can feel activating and frightening. Even an impulse of an emotion can evoke the feeling of lack of safety, or danger. If as a child you didn't feel safe to feel and express your emotions, this adds to the feeling that emotions are dangerous. Fearful that they could engulf you, you pushed them down, repressed, or dissociated. Unresolved, this limits your experience of life. Without emotions, at best you are only partially living your life, and your heart remains closed to some degree.

Using tremendous amounts of your life force energy to keep unbearable feelings and emotions outside of your awareness is truly exhausting. *Not feeling* once served you to ensure your sense of survival, but it no longer does.

AN INNER CONFLICT ABOUT FEELING

The emotions of anger, rage, shame, grief, guilt, deep sadness, and loss that often stem from trauma, rather than being an exquisite expression of your humanness, can be terrifying, so they're shut away, distorted, and rejected. These repressed emotions work against you. The inner conflict between the need to express them and the need to deny them is exhausting and often has an associated negative belief.

Are you aware of any internal conflicts about expressing emotion or inner quandaries that leave you feeling stuck? Be curious rather than judgmental. Notice what you feel in your body. Any patterns or adaptations you uncover are survival strategies, so be as gentle or compassionate toward yourself as possible.

Consider the following examples of inner conflicts and quandaries about emotions and underline the ones that apply to you. There is space to describe others that you come up with now or later.

- I know I'm sad yet am afraid to feel sad, as it will overwhelm and consume me.

- If I feel emotion I will fall apart.

- I'm angry, but I'm afraid if I express anger I'll become like my father/mother.

- If I express sadness I will be rejected, so I don't express my sadness, but then I feel rejected anyway.

- If I show my feelings I won't be loved—yet people don't show me love, as I don't show my feelings.

- I'm numb to emotions; even though I'd like to feel them, I'm afraid to.

- When I feel emotion it feels scary, so I stop feeling.

- When I feel angry, I also feel I'm not supposed to.

- I'm afraid if I get angry I'll hurt someone or myself.

- If I express emotions with any assertiveness, I won't be loved.

- Part of me feels happy; another part of me feels afraid to be happy.

- As soon as I feel joy, I need to shut it down.

- _____

- _____

- _____

How does it feel to acknowledge any internal conflicts? Can you describe your experience?

_____

_____

Can you identify when and/or why each conflict/belief first came into existence? For instance, as an adult Catherine felt a threat any time a positive emotion surfaced within her. She had never explored why; she kept her thoughts about it at bay. It was simply too scary, and consequently her life felt very limited. Once she began to explore trauma, and with support, she looked closely at the internal dynamics.

Catherine realized that when she was very young her mother had no patience for her joyous expressions. Once, as Catherine danced around the living room, her mother slapped her violently. It was so shocking, frightening, and confusing that Catherine decided to keep joy hidden forever.

She felt there was something wrong with expressing joy or happiness.

Expressing joy meant losing love.

This child aspect of Catherine's consciousness was still hiding her joy and happiness, still feeling unsafe to express these emotions in adulthood.

With a greater sense of agency that she had built through other practices, Catherine was able to face the fear and tolerate the inner conflict. As she did, she felt expansion and profound relief. She could feel the conflict diminish. At first she felt uncertainty, yet with encouragement she trusted her body's capacity to organize itself.

Resolving inner conflicts often comes about when you can hold the opposing views or feelings. This dissolves the conflict at a visceral level. You must first be grounded in your body enough to bear the internal conflict; then you can ease the mental struggle so your mind can hold the opposites.

In the following exercise, the idea is to hold the conflicting beliefs simultaneously. For Catherine this meant allowing herself to simultaneously feel joy and the fear of feeling joy.

EXERCISE: Resolving Inner Conflicts

1. Seated comfortably, ground yourself in your body and become as present as you can in this moment.

2. Recall an inner conflict that you're ready to face and resolve.

3. If this conflict arose from either an incident in childhood or an acute trauma, hold a compassionate view for both the one who was hurt and your adult perspective as the one present right now.

4. As you feel your conflicting emotions or beliefs, simply remain present and curious. You may feel the contraction of the conflict begin to dissolve. By feeling the opposites, the tension will soften over time, freeing your life energy.

5. Stay with the sensation in your body and observe any changes as you feel. You're integrating your past as you anchor the feelings in your body.

Describe what it was like for you to explore inner conflicts and quandaries around your emotions. What did you discover about yourself, and your beliefs? Did you have any insights? What felt and feels different now? Especially notice the area of your chest and heart; how does that feel? How does it feel to acknowledge your experience without judgment?

_____

_____

_____

_____

_____

_____

YOUR EMOTIONAL CUES AND BOUNDARIES

The job of your primary caregivers was to bring you into being and contribute to your development both emotionally and psychologically. In the first twelve or so years of your life, you looked to your caregivers for your emotional cues. Your relationship with them built the foundation that determined your relationship with emotions—yours and others. Your experiences with your caregivers in those years directly affect how you feel and express your emotions later in life.

Take a moment to consider the following questions and circle your answers:

- Were your parents or primary caregivers living with unresolved trauma?   Yes   No   Unsure

- Were your caregivers abusive, withdrawn, neglectful, or explosive at times?   Yes   No

- Did your caregivers deny their own emotions or hide them from you?   Yes   No

- Did your caregivers quarrel a lot and frighten you?   Yes   No

- Did they tell you to not be angry or sad, to not cry?   Yes   No

- Do you remember closing down your joy or your anger around your parents?   Yes   No

- Were you born in a time of revolution, unrest, war, or economic depression?   Yes   No

- Were you brought up at a time when your caregivers were stressed, especially in your early life?   Yes   No   Unsure

If you answered yes to any of these questions, you likely have not developed the internal navigation system you need to feel fully connected to and comfortable with emotions—your own and others—and your relationship to emotions may have gone askew and your capacity to respond to challenging situations in an emotionally healthy way could be limited.

EXERCISE: Your Emotions in Childhood

Take a moment to remember your experiences with emotions as a child. The following questions are prompts to help you remember. If you don't remember your childhood experience, relate the questions to your present self and your close relationships (which tend to reflect your early relationships).

Part 1

- What happened if you got angry as a child? For example, was your anger accepted? Were you guided to express it healthily? Were you told off? Did you fear feeling angry? Were you told that being angry was okay? Did you feel loved and accepted or rejected?

  _____

  _____

  _____

- Recall an experience of being angry and describe it. Be aware of your body as you remember and write. Pause when you feel something within your body, so you acknowledge your body's response. If you feel any anger now, remain present with it. If you can witness the anger and not become overwhelmed, you are reintegrating your life force. Integrating anger gently transforms this energy back into a sense of internal power.

  _____

  _____

  _____

- Do you remember other feelings associated with your feeling angry; for example, shame or sadness? Describe how other feelings were for you, and how they are now as you remember.

  _____

  _____

  _____

- What was it like for you when you were sad as a child? For instance, when you were sad, did your parents stay with you, allowing you to be sad? Did they hold you? Did they help you experience and move through the emotion? Did you feel ignored or alone when sad? Did you hide your sadness?

  _____

  _____

  _____

- How did it feel to be asked how you felt—or *not* asked?

  _____

  _____

- How did it feel to explore emotions in your body with your caregivers? Or how did it feel when you did not?

  _____

  _____

- Were you ever told not to feel, even in what may have seemed a caring way—for instance, "Don't cry, everything will be fine"?   **Yes   No**

- Describe what was this like for you.

  _____

  _____

  _____

- If you got upset at your caregivers, even momentarily, did they let you know that it was normal—that they loved you anyway? Or did they get angry or upset and tell you it wasn't okay to feel that way? Or did you keep your feelings hidden and withdraw to your room? Write about an experience of feeling upset with your caregivers, how it felt for you, and their response.

_____

_____

_____

- Do you remember what happened when you cried? Did your caregivers allow you to cry, or did they try to stop you? Write about a time you remember crying and your caregivers' response.

_____

_____

_____

Part 2

- Describe your family's overall relationship to emotions. Describe any insights or observations from part one. For instance, do you recognize any patterns or beliefs regarding your emotional expression that no longer serve you? Once you see a belief or a pattern you are no longer subject to it and can better create change and transformation.

_____

_____

_____

- Describe your current overall relationship to emotions, particularly greater capacity to feel your emotions since you were a child, and any greater emotional capacity since beginning this workbook.

_____

_____

_____

EMOTIONS IN INFANCY

As you explore your emotions, it's important to review developmental trauma in infancy and early childhood, to see if the root cause happened then. You don't have to remember, or revisit, but having information can help you understand what essential needs may have been unmet. Remember, trauma doesn't arise only from a traumatic event, but emerges within us when necessary elements were missing—nurturance, holding, attunement, or a calm loving presence.

Crying It Out

A current cultural misperception says that leaving babies alone to cry themselves to sleep is appropriate and good parenting.[49] Although to many this may appear to be a nonthreatening approach to caregiving, research has shown that without timely intervention the infant's brain will be flooded with high levels of potentially neurotoxic stress hormones.[50] This form of isolation negatively influences the development of brain systems and the neurochemistry that allows for healthy interpersonal relationships.[51]

An infant doesn't have the capacity to self-soothe. Leaving a baby alone to cry for extended periods can damage its well-being and trigger dissociation, which can become a default pattern in adulthood.[52] The ability to self-soothe and self-regulate is developed over the course of infancy through the calm holding, nurturing, and attending presence of a loving parental figure. This develops the infant's healthy neurophysiology and capacity for intimacy, especially in the first six to twelve months.

Parental Stress and Anxiety

Caregivers who themselves are anxious, depressed, or fearful, or have unresolved trauma, or lack the capacity to be fully present and calm with their children pass on similar states of dysregulation in their child's nervous system and body. Your brain develops in interaction with the environment. For instance, if a mother is stressed, this deeply affects the developing brain of her fetus or infant, creating physiological dysregulation, with psychological repercussions. Research indicates that relational trauma with caregivers alters right brain development, which creates a predisposition for difficulties with forming a healthy sense of self or agency, and personality challenges and disorders later in life.[53] Your early developing right brain, which is formed by your early caregiver relationship, is deeply connected to the ANS and shapes healthy functioning of the sympathetic and parasympathetic nervous systems, which determine your adult social and emotional capacities.[54] Even the most loving and attentive caregivers can be inhibited in sharing their love and presence due to their own unresolved trauma. The traumatized child' dissociated emotion and vibrant life energy are bound in the body and nervous system in the form of undischarged arousal, held as physical tensions and other somatizations.[55] That said, you can alter the effects of a less-than-optimal early relational experience by attending to your body, cultivating body awareness, restoring healthy whole-brain functioning, and recalibrating your ANS by practicing the exercises in this workbook.

PAUSE FOR REFLECTION: An Initial Look at Developmental Trauma

Consider these questions and circle your answers.

- Did your parents leave you to *cry it out*? Yes No

- Was your primary caregiver anxious, depressed, fearful, traumatized, or disconnected? Yes No

- Did your caregiver undergo a traumatic experience when you were very young, such as the loss of a spouse or parent, or major surgery? Yes No

If you answered yes to any of these questions, does this make sense in terms of your current symptoms of trauma?

Exploring very early trauma can be upsetting. Even if you don't directly remember this form of trauma, your body may. Be gentle and loving with yourself if any discomfort arises. Imagine you can sense that infant consciousness that was so scared; imagine yourself being soothing and loving in a way you lacked back then. Imagine bringing the image of your young self into your heart center; hold the child closely as you gently rock and soothe it. As you do so, you're attending to your own needs. Spend as much time with this imaginative exercise as you can; it can be powerfully transformative.

Your brain has an inherent flexibility to adjust and change, called *neuroplasticity*. This allows you to develop and recover healthier, more productive and loving ways of relating to yourself, others, and the world.

Describe here any feeling or insights on this topic so far. As you continue reading, come back to this space and add what you learn about yourself.

_____

_____

_____

_____

_____

_____

_____

_____

ADAPTING TO DIFFICULT CONDITIONS

If your essential needs were not met as an infant or child, default behavior that you automatically go to in stressful situations later in life may have become ingrained response patterns and you may

- Feel yourself dissociating in situations that are not particularly frightening

- Fear being rejected or abandoned, or feel you were

- Reject others, or reject and abandon yourself, never really attuning to yourself

- Have foreclosed your own needs, as it was too painful to not have them met

- Have learned to cut yourself off from emotions, as they felt unbearable when you weren't attended to

- Have disconnected from your body and ability to feel your embodied life force

- Have foreclosed your heart's openness to love, feeling that loss of love is too painful to ever bear again

And all of this can remain outside of your awareness.

The pain of not having your needs met as a child is incredibly distressing and creates numerous negative beliefs about yourself, others, and the world. Your adaptations or strategies to survive these painful times are likely still haunting your life. Fortunately, through our exploration together and the exercises you're doing, you'll find insight into the necessary but missing elements of life force and find ways to bring them into your life now, creating new neuronal networks and connections, with restored feelings of love, safety, and connection.

SELF-CHECK-IN: WHAT DO I NEED?

As an adult you can attend to your needs or at least acknowledge them. If they cannot be met, you'll be okay. A child's not having their needs met can feel like a life threat and trigger the impulse to disconnect or to shut down. In this case, expressing your needs became connected to the loss of your caregiver, instigating a psychological response to diminish or foreclose them. You may experience shame or feelings of badness around having needs. If you suffered with your needs not been met as a child or in any trauma, simply acknowledging your needs now can recalibrate your nervous system and feel very soothing. If you foreclosed your needs, your initial work is to begin knowing what they are. As you learn about trauma and your response, you're empowering yourself with other options.

Once you know your needs, you may be able to meet them; for instance, if you feel like you need to be held and soothed, you can place your hands on your opposite shoulders and give yourself a hug. Part of healing trauma is to give your body what it didn't receive at the time of the traumatic event/s.

CULTIVATING DUAL AWARENESS

It is crucial, as you do this work, that you're aware of both your adult self and traumatized child consciousness and don't regress into a child state. The idea is to integrate any consciousness that was split off or dissociated, not to reify an inner child. This is a form of dual awareness. Regressing fully into an early state is retraumatizing; you may have a deep cathartic expression of emotion, but no integrative healing takes place. Any time you're aware that your early or child consciousness is present, you need to be grounded in your adult self and connected, to some degree, to your body awareness.

Practice the following exercise any time you feel upset, distressed or out of sorts in any way.

EXERCISE: Tending to Your Needs

1. Take a moment to connect with yourself, your inner experience. Do you need anything right now?

2. What signals let you know you need something? It could be an impulse, feeling, emotion, or intuitive sense.

3. What do you need? You might want to be held, or, some other form of comfort; you may want to feel safe, to yell or disconnect, to breathe deeply, to be nourished or nurtured.

4. If you know what you need, complete this sentence. *In this moment, I need:*

    _____

    _____

5. If you don't know, complete this sentence: *When I don't know what I need, I feel:*

    _____

    _____

If you're in touch with an essential need right now, use your imagination or one or more of the exercises that you've learned to create the internal conditions so that you can give yourself what you need in this moment. (If you need to scream, do so only in your imagination.)

- Try simply wrapping your arms around your shoulders to hug yourself.

- Notice your breath and any softening in your body.

Be gentle with yourself. As a child, when your needs weren't met, it probably felt very threatening. As an adult, you have many more resources to get your needs met. And if you must wait, be aware that as an adult, not having the need met is not life-threatening. And as you evoke your old identifications—such as badness or fear—versus the reality of the moment, you can begin to dis-identify from them.

TIME TO SELF-SOOTHE

In this self-soothing exercise, you'll create a prolonged sound as you exhale that will gently resonate in different areas of your body. The slight vibration activates your vagus nerve, a long sinewy nerve that innervates the surfaces of your larynx and laryngopharynx and interfaces with the parasympathetic control of your lungs, heart, and digestive tract, providing visceral sensation. The slight airway resistance and vibration increase vagal tone and brings physiological relaxation while deactivating your limbic system, the part of your brain involved in emotions such as fear, anger, pleasure, and instinctual drives.[56] This practice gently allows your breath to penetrate and release body tensions.

EXERCISE: The Sound of Aum (Om)

This is a wonderful exercise to do any time you feel anxious or upset. Read the entire exercise before you begin. Do only three Aum breaths in a session so as not to overstimulate your system, but feel free to practice many times a day.

1. Sit in a posture with an upright spine, slightly lowering your chin to lengthen the back of your neck.

2. Exhale completely.

3. Beginning as deep in your belly as possible, take in a deep breath—allow your belly to fill, then your lower rib cage, all the way up to your upper chest. (If your breath doesn't fully expand your belly yet, don't worry. Many people who've experienced trauma have a tight diaphragm, which blocks this. This exercise can help to relax your diaphragm to allow for deeper breathing.)

4. As you exhale, slightly purse your lips and create the long-extended sound of Aum (sounds like Om), until your exhale is complete.

5. Allow your body to take a full inhalation and repeat the extended sound of Aum.

6. Repeat three times.

7. Sit in stillness, noticing your body's response to the sound and vibration. Do you feel any softening, tingling, relaxation?

BREATH HELPS REGULATE EMOTION

There is a wonderful reciprocal relationship between your emotions and breathing. Your breath is a major tool that helps with emotional regulation. You can use breathing exercises to help you self-regulate when difficult emotions and insights emerge. For instance, it can be truly crushing to fully realize that you feel bad about yourself, even if it's been true for years. Your breath and life force can help you calm and ready yourself for assimilation, integration, and change.

When your breath is not flowing optimally, you're not feeling the full and natural flow of life energy. Holding tension, your body can become increasingly tight and rigid, and your emotions can also become fixed or frozen. Breathing exercises can be a wonderful ally in helping you tolerate more emotion and lessening overwhelming emotions.

Research shows that to cope, traumatized people learn to shut down the brain areas that transmit the visceral feelings and emotions that convey and portray fear and terror; instead, they numb and disconnect.[57] However, the fear and terror still affect them. Being able to tolerate the visceral experience of emotion—from your inner organs, especially the gut—is essential for resolving trauma and creating permanent positive changes in your life. Wisely using your breath and life force will help you reconnect to feeling and help you tolerate visceral sensations and emotions.

FEELING YOUR LIFE FORCE

As you regain access to a wider spectrum of emotions, you can feel life force energy moving through your body. The next exercise helps you tap into this vital force.

The roots of this exercise trace back to ancient China and the discovery of the body's meridian lines—channels in which life force (chi) flows. There are both Eastern and Western medical interpretations of the meridians' function in practices such as acupuncture and tapping, or acupressure. I've included enough information to make sense of the exercise and connect it in the context of healing trauma.

By simply tapping certain body areas related to the meridians' energy flow, you're connecting with your body's subtle energy system. As you tap your body, signals relay safety to your brain, so you can soften. As you gently tap, you stimulate the movement of energy, and over time develop the capability to tolerate more energy flow and sensation, you cultivate your capacity to feel more intense emotion.

EXERCISE: Tapping for Life and Energy Flow

This exercise helps you become more comfortable with the sensation of energy—life force moving in your body. This is important; the more comfortable you become with this, the more you can tolerate emotion. Stand *or* sit for the exercise. You can tap as lightly or as strongly as you feel comfortable, using your fist.

1. Begin by tapping from the top of your shoulder down the outside of your arm, to the back of your hand, then rotate your arm and tap from the palm up the inside of your arm. Repeat this a few times, then do the same for the other arm.

2. Immediately afterward, pause and feel the sensations.

3. Now tap your legs. Beginning at the outside of your hip, tap all the way down to the ankle and then up the inside of your leg. Repeat a couple of times and then tap the other leg.

4. Pause and notice the energy and sensations. How does it feel?

5. If it's comfortable, you can try tapping your scalp and shoulders and across your chest. Pause and feel the sensations.

Experiment gently with this exercise. You may improve energy flow that has been disrupted or blocked from trauma, as well as enhancing your capacity to feel more. If the stimulation feels like too much, firmly rub your hands across the areas you tapped.

By cultivating more body awareness and observation skills, you'll become aware of *implicit* memories and the behaviors and impulses driven by them. By observing, you keep your prefrontal cortex, or executive functioning engaged, which prevents overwhelm. Awareness, insight, and observing lead to a renegotiation in your whole system.

LIFE FORCE, SPIRITUALITY, AND EMOTION

Healing trauma at its core is spiritual as it nurtures a transformation of consciousness and a fuller embodiment of your authentic self. You're connecting all the elements of your being, including your emotions, into a coherent sense of wholeness. Your human birthright is to be able to feel and tolerate a whole range of emotions. The exercises in this book help you develop an embodied spiritual practice tailored to your needs, desires, and healthy emotional expression. Spirituality does not dismiss any emotion. You want to cultivate the capacity to allow emotion to flow through you, to not become stuck.

Do you currently have a spiritual practice or belief that helps you deal with the consequences of trauma and embraces your capacity for feeling emotion?   **Yes**   **No**

- If yes, describe here how it helps you with resolving trauma and feeling emotion.

  _____

  _____

- If no, reflect on what you've experienced in the exercises you've done. Have you experienced a deeper connection with yourself? With something greater than yourself?

  _____

  _____

Now describe a practice that enhances your sense of spirituality, if you have one, or if you don't, reflect on your experiences with the exercises so far. Remember, spirituality is not limited to old ideas or dogmas or beliefs; it lives in you and through you, expressing your most essential nature in an embodied and authentic way. And your emotional states—even anger, which you'll be exploring more—are deeply connected to your sense of self and spirituality. Anger is your life force energy, often distorted into unhealthy expressions that turn inward or lash outward. You're developing the capacity to shift the distorted energy of unresolved emotions back into the flow of your life force, which connects you with the energy of the cosmos.

_____

_____

_____

_____

_____

_____

WHAT I'VE LEARNED ABOUT EMOTIONS, LIFE FORCE, AND SPIRITUALITY

Looking back on your reading of this chapter and trying out the exercises, can you see how your life force, emotions, and spirituality are not separate experiences or expressions of your being? So many of us tend to compartmentalize these areas. You're deconstructing those walls within you—and compassion spans all the dimensions of your being. How is your experience of compassion changing or deepening?

Describe any insights and what may be most relevant for you now.

_____

_____

_____

_____

_____

_____

CHAPTER 7

Navigating Emotional Overwhelm with Healthy Boundaries

In loving, you risk being denied love. This may explain your unconscious resistance to the intimacy of freely loving others, and self-love. You're working on dissolving that resistance and the emotional anguish surrounding it. And if someone can't return the love you desire, as an adult you have more choices than when you were a child, when perceiving the loss of love was unbearable. It's most important to know *you are* love. The disconnection caused by early trauma prevents your feeling the fullness of the love of your heart and emotions. Opening to love is a gesture of vulnerability and a surrender to your spiritual needs. Developmental or shock trauma can leave you feeling unworthy, lacking self-esteem, shameful and unlovable, which leads to feelings of rejection and the rejection of love. Just as a caterpillar transforms into a butterfly, healing trauma releases you from the confines of your isolating cocoon, allowing you to find and connect or reconnect with your essence and to experience greater freedom to feel life's myriad expressions, especially love.

Allowing yourself what was once denied by others or you felt was missing as a child can paradoxically feel painful. When you take active control of your attention, your awareness expands and the prefrontal circuitry (prefrontal cortex) of your brain is activated and comes "online," helping that emotional pain to flow through you so you can transform into that metaphorical butterfly.

THE EXECUTIVE FUNCTION OF YOUR BRAIN AND YOUR EMOTIONS

Psychologists use "executive function" to describe the role of the prefrontal cortex in relationship to the rest of your brain and body. The prefrontal cortex is where thinking and emotions converge. Your executive function oversees abstract thinking, thought analysis, decision making, and social behavior, enabling you to repress inadvisable urges such as angry outbursts. Your executive function can also quiet your amygdala (two small almond-shaped structures, one in each side of the brain).

The amygdala is responsible for autonomic responses associated with fear. They act like radar, alerting your brain when they perceive something significantly dangerous happening. When you're subjected to someone's anger or facing a threat, or during a traumatic event, the amygdala is activated; its signal puts you on alert. If the threat seems urgent, the amygdala engages other brain circuitry, enabling the best and most adaptive response.

YOUR PAST IN THE PRESENT

Your amygdala may react to danger based on *past experience*, not the *present situation*. Sensing a threat in the present, the amygdala triggers the hypothalamic-pituitary-adrenal axis—your central stress response system—hijacking your executive functioning until the perceived threat is gone. When this happens, you're plunged into a survival mode of fight, flight, or freeze.

As information is relayed to the amygdala, another, slightly slower brain response takes place as information also goes to your higher-brain structures, of which the prefrontal cortex is a part. This system is like a second opinion that can interpret what's happening by using memory and association. It will whether a threat truly exists. If no threat is perceived, the amygdala is directed to calm down, and your system self-regulates—no need to fight, flee, or freeze.

However, if well-worn pathways in your ANS have developed due to unresolved past trauma, your higher-brain structures can't "convince" the lower-brain structures that there is no present threat. Your neural network can also develop a default mechanism of withdrawal or dissociation due to trauma. Then your body will respond as if there is still a threat. In both instances, your lower brain can't "hear" the higher brain or override the preconditioned fear and emotional impulses.

When you've experienced trauma, your brain learns to recognize characteristics of your trauma experience as warning signals. These could be smells, sounds, or colors. Whether innate or learned, when these signals are present, they can cause your amygdala cells to fire rapidly. Your response may not be matched to your current environment. As you explore and resolve trauma, the integration process you're assimilating helps foster your best functioning in your present and anticipated future.[58]

PAUSE FOR REFLECTION: **When Emotions Overwhelm You**

Can you think of a time when you were *hijacked* by your emotions, or you overreacted to a situation and were surprised by the intensity of your reactions, especially your emotions? Or that you froze when you knew you weren't in actual danger? Describe what happened.

_____

_____

_____

How did you feel about yourself afterward? Did you

• Feel ashamed or embarrassed?	Yes	No
• Become self-critical?	Yes	No
• Feel compassion for yourself?	Yes	No
• Blame others for your response?	Yes	No
• Feel angry at yourself?	Yes	No
• Feel angry at others?	Yes	No
• Apologize afterward?	Yes	No
• Disconnect and not think about it afterward?	Yes	No
• Experience intrusive thoughts about the incident afterward?	Yes	No

Record how it was for you emotionally in the moment, and how you feel now as you recall it.

_____

_____

_____

In answering the questions, do you recognize where you are self-critical—or kind? Do you feel that with greater understanding of what happens in an *emotional hijack,* you may be able to be kinder to yourself? Write an example.

_____

_____

_____

If you notice self-judgments, practice cultivating compassion.

EMOTIONAL OVERWHELM

Imagine looking through a window to your garden. You would like to sit out there to relax; however, it has been unattended for a while. It's overgrown with weeds, stinging nettle, and poison oak, and strewn with windblown trash. It feels like simply too much to attend to. Looking at it gives you a constant feeling of overwhelm. You could close your drapes to feel better, but it's still there, bothering you at some level, and you're preventing the fullness of day-light from entering. You may well feel the same way about your emotions: overwhelmed at the prospect of tackling them, so you "close the drapes" to shut them out.

Sometimes just feeling an emotion is overwhelming. It connects you to that whole unattended garden of emotion, so you try to avoid it even more—which may work for a while, or occasionally overwhelm you.

The purpose of this next exercise is to learn which emotions may overwhelm you, or which emotions you may avoid. Or maybe someone else's emotion triggers you—upsetting you or hurting your feelings. You will learn to tend to these emotions with greater ease.

EXERCISE: Assessment of Emotional Overwhelm

- Are some emotions more likely to overwhelm you? For instance, anger, rage, sadness, shame, or grief?

- Observing your body, what happens when you think about these emotions now?

  _____

  _____

  _____

- Can you describe what happens when you're with someone who is expressing these emotions? What is your response? Do you leave the room, try and stop the emotions, dissociate?

  _____

  _____

  _____

- Is there an emotion that you tend to feel when you're upset or triggered? For instance, do you move easily into sadness but not anger, or vice versa?

  _____

  _____

  _____

- If you're aware of having one go-to emotion, could this be a way to avoid another emotion that was once too unbearable or frightening to feel?

DEVELOPING EMOTIONAL AWARENESS

You may want to start a journal about emotional responses that overwhelm you:

- What situations or people are triggers that upset you?

- How do you feel in response to others triggering you?

- What do you do in response?

- What other things about your responses do you notice as you develop your emotional awareness? Be very specific about what is upsetting about the situation or person.

_____

_____

_____

- When you check in with yourself, are you aware of any of the following?

  - This pattern goes on with your relationship to yourself.

  - You yourself do or could do what this other person does that triggers you, and you're just beginning to realize this.

  - You're quite capable of the attitude or action you find triggering or offensive and haven't come to terms with this yet.

- Continuing the check-in, could you have another perception or understanding, given your deepening understanding of what triggers you?

- Further, as you realize that many human reactions arise from adaptations to difficult situations, can you practice compassion for yourself and your responses, and see if another more compassionate perception of the situation emerges?

- Describe, with compassion, any insights you have about what triggered you.

_____

_____

Recognizing what you're experiencing and that you're out of balance in some way is a powerful tool. The more awareness you bring to your emotions and reactions, the more easily you can feel and change your relationship to them.

In the context of this book, developing your awareness means observing what goes on in your inner terrain—your processes and reactions. It's allowing you to observe what is occurring with curiosity—and less judgment. You're creating more inner space, which allows repressed or forgotten experiences to gently come into your awareness. When you're observing, your executive functioning is online, and you're less likely to be overwhelmed by experiences. Instead of reacting, you're responding and promoting self-healing.

EMBODYING A RANGE OF EMOTIONS

In your healing journey, you'll become able to tolerate both negative and positive emotions. Emotions in themselves are not good or bad. They are but a variety of expressions that humans experience. Being able to tolerate a wide range of emotions is essential to increasing your capacity for resilience, joy, and love, and living as full a life as possible. Sadness, joy, grief, love, anger—all are to be embraced.

Healing, again, is often discontinuous and labyrinthine. Your brain moves from organization to disorganization and back to organization, each time establishing *higher levels* of organization with established presence and awareness.

The following exercise will help you develop resilience, emotional regulation, and an inner pliancy that allows you to shift easily between emotions, to prevent getting *stuck* as you work through your trauma. (An audio recording of instructions for this exercise is available at http://www.newharbinger.com/43256.)

EXERCISE: Flow of Opposite Emotions

This exercise cultivates your capacity for emotional pliancy and wisdom.

1. Begin in a comfortable seated or reclining position. Be aware of your body as a field of sensation, or simply notice your whole body, even if parts feel disconnected or numb.

2. Recall a time when you felt happy. Notice all the sensations in your body connected with happiness. Remember as many related details as possible. Maybe your face, chest, or belly feel lighter? Stay with the experience for a minute or so. Where in your body do you feel the happiness? How deeply? What texture is it?

3. Now recall in detail a time when you felt sad. Notice what happens in your body. Keep observing; keep being curious. How do your chest and throat feel? Where do you notice sadness in your body?

4. Return to the memory of being happy, and stay with the sensations connected to happiness for a minute or so. Anchor them deeply in the felt sense of your body.

You can go back and forth several times and try different emotional states: excitement and dread, joy and grief, calmness and anger. Eventually, you may notice a state within your body, a resolution of tension between these states that emerges as stillness. If so, rest in the stillness. Experiencing this may or may not take many practice sessions.

DEVELOPING ROBUST BOUNDARIES PREVENTS EMOTIONAL OVERWHELM

Appropriate boundaries are an important part of any relationship. Boundaries get ruptured in trauma. Your skin is your most obvious boundary. In physical trauma your skin may tear open, requiring you tend to it with bandages and possibly stitches. You have another boundary that is energetic; one not as obvious, as it's immaterial. Like your skin, this boundary can be ruptured by trauma.

Though it's invisible, you can sense this energetic boundary—perhaps as a knowing when a person is in your personal space, too close for comfort. This energetic boundary is as necessary as your skin for overall well-being. By being more aware of it and having it function optimally, you can feel more confident in your authentic expression and safe in expressing emotion.

Before you explore this boundary further, consider some of the indications that your energetic boundary has been ruptured. Underline what applies to you.

- I'm *hyper*sensitive to light, sound, and other stimuli.

- I alternate between not feeling much and being flooded by stimuli.

- I have poor boundary enforcement with others, such as finding it difficult to say *no*, or allowing others into my personal space when I would rather they not be there.

- I have difficulty setting limits.

- I'm extremely sensitive to other people's emotions.

- I have difficulty knowing the difference between myself and others.

- I have poor perception of others' boundaries. I'm not aware of their personal space.

- I sense that danger can come from anywhere at any time.

- I feel raw, like I'm walking around without skin.

- I feel exhausted after interacting with some people.

Creating and intentionally setting healthy boundaries is not only a form of self-care and a means of creating healthier relationships; it strengthens your capacity to heal from trauma. Healthy boundaries give you a safe, defined space in which it becomes easier to set and know your limits. Boundaries allow you to know what you want and how to express that and to safely experience your emotions. The best way to learn about your energetic boundaries is to experience them yourself. Having healthy energetic boundaries means:

- You can say no when you want to and set limits.

- You know the difference between yourself and another person.

- You feel comfortable in your body.

- You don't feel flooded by other people's emotional states or neediness.

- You inherently feel safe in your body and in the world.

- You feel comfortable in crowded places.

- You can distinguish between your emotions and others'.

In the process of creating and setting good boundaries, you're also creating the capability to set better limits for yourself. When you are able to, acknowledge the reasons why you haven't been able to do this, using the self-compassion practices you've learned here.

The difficulty in setting limits likely arose from your caregivers or surroundings that failed to give you what you needed as a child to feel completely safe to say no, or failed to offer good examples of boundary setting, or failed to let you know you had a right to set limits for yourself. Or maybe you suffered a terrible violation or ruptured boundaries in a shock trauma. This next exercise is for your inquiry to give you some insight for the exercise that follows it.

Note that a feeling of frustration or anger may arise now as a naturally aggressive impulse in response to your recognizing needing to retract your boundaries or having them ruptured in the past. And anger is natural if you were violated in any way. Anger arises for resolution—it can be a good sign of a protest you couldn't express during the traumatic experience—yet it may feel frightening. If you're not yet ready to feel the aggressive impulse or anger in your body, go to the previous exercise of opposite emotions and work with anger and calm, or to other exercises that help you build your capacity to feel more sensation and life force energy.

EXERCISE: Setting Healthy Limits

1. Take a meditative or self-inquiring posture—sit upright with a lengthened spine, keeping the back of your neck long by having your chin level. Take a few deep breaths with complete exhales and set an intention for dissolving any limiting beliefs.

2. You're inquiring into why your boundaries are not strong and why you have difficulty setting limits. Spend a few moments with each of these possibilities. As you read them, simply notice your body, thoughts, emotions, feelings, and images to help give you some insight.

   • I had difficulty telling a parent no or stop.

   • My parents didn't show good boundaries with me.

   • If I say no, I will be abandoned.

   • If I say no, I will be rejected.

   • If I set limits, I will be abandoned.

   • If I set limits, I will be rejected.

   • If I set limits, I won't be liked or loved.

   • I'm afraid I'll be alone if I say no.

   • I was hurt in a shock trauma and am still hurting.

3. Write down your responses.

   _____

   _____

   _____

As you feel any responses to these statements, be aware that these may be connected to old beliefs that limit your current life. As an adult developing a strong sense of agency—confidence, inner strength, knowing who you are in the world—you have many more choices now and are developing capacities to make other responses as you stand in your truth and set limits. To do so, you may first need to create a strong boundary.

In the following exercise, you'll need something with which you can create a circle. A hula hoop or two long scarves placed in a circle shape will work. You may also want to place a chair or stool in the center of the circle if you're not comfortable sitting on the floor.

EXERCISE: Creating a Strong and Flexible Boundary

Part 1

1. Create your circle on the floor around you.

2. Standing outside of the circle, notice how you're feeling and your relationship to the space around you.

3. Step into your circle and sit down. Again notice your relationship to the space around you. Notice how you feel physically and the containment that the circle provides. Spend a few moments exploring the subtlety of sensations and feelings.

4. Remain sitting and quickly remove the circle from around you.

5. Notice how your body feels and again notice your relationship to the space around you.

6. Again place the circle around you. Notice how you feel now.

7. Now imagine your energetic boundary is an egg shape that surrounds your whole body. You may imagine this boundary is made of a protective light, gold, or guardians. Be creative! Imagine a boundary made of anything that allows you to feel safe within it.

Many people find it easier to feel their body when they sit within their imagined energetic boundary. Notice whether this is true for you, right now and whenever you do this exercise. The more you imagine your boundary, the stronger your energetic boundary becomes. Eventually you'll no longer need to use the physical circle.

Part 2

1. Sit on the floor in your circle. Notice how you feel physically and emotionally.

2. Sense your boundary. Now imagine it as an egg shape surrounding you.

3. Begin to sense if and where there is a tear, weak area, or rupture in the boundary. For example, your boundary may feel less strong behind you. Or, let's say you were hit on your left side in a traumatic event; there may be an impairment in the boundary there. Be sure to check in front of you, behind you, on each side, and above your head and beneath you.

4. Each time you find an area that needs repair, work to strengthen it. Using your imagination, visualize reinforcing your boundary. It might take the form of stitches or a gold plate or be a particular color.

I recommend sitting inside your physically encircled boundary for a few minutes every day until you can sense it energetically without using whatever you've chosen to represent it. Simply feeling your boundary and imagining it *will* reestablish it. In addition to using this physical boundary to experience and repair it as you have in these two exercises, you can use your physical boundary in other situations.

Cynthia used her hula hoop boundary every time she spoke on the phone with her mother, with whom she did not have good boundaries. Cynthia always felt exhausted after a call. She also lost any sense of whose emotions she was experiencing, hers or her mother's. But sitting inside her hula hoop, Cynthia felt stronger and more confident. She didn't get pulled into her old patterns of caretaking her mother's needs. She could say no. She could differentiate her emotions from her mother's.

Do you experience someone in your life in a similar way? Try sitting inside your boundary during a phone call. See if you feel stronger and more confident, or have an easier time saying no or a clearer sense of *your* body, *your* needs, and *your* emotions.

Saying No

No is a basic boundary-setting word. Being clear and concise with your no is important in your healing process as it reestablishes your boundaries, your sense of self-control, and your personal limits. People with poor boundaries have difficulty saying no to others' demands or to their own internal pressure, falling prey to their inner *I should*.

The following exercise is quite powerful, so take care and go slowly. It may bring up some deep emotions. Always remember the resources you've created for yourself and return to them whenever you need to. With each step you take, with every new awareness, you're creating greater resilience, aliveness, and wisdom. Stay connected to the felt sense of your body. Sometimes putting your hands out in front of you, palms facing forward, creates a stronger boundary.

EXERCISE: No!

1. Sit in your boundary circle if this helps you to feel safer.

2. Once you've established the feeling or sense of your boundary, repeat the word "no" three times and then pause.

3. Notice your body. Notice how you feel. Be very curious. What sensations do you notice? How is your breathing affected? Do you notice any emotion?

4. Say "no" three more times. Pause after each no for a few seconds so you can feel the effects. Notice the tone of your voice. Is your no clear and emphatic or timid, hesitant, more a question than a statement?

5. If your no! isn't strong, clear and concise, see if you can ground yourself more deeply in your body. Say it again: "no, no, no." Pause and see how you feel. Make sure you're breathing. Be curious about your whole experience.

6. Once again, say "no, no, no." Notice your experience.

7. Describe your experience and how you feel now.

_____

_____

_____

_____

_____

_____

You can use this exercise saying the word "stop." You may find that your arm wants to come up with the palm of your hand facing forward.

Describe your experience. Note the differences between saying no and saying stop.

_____

_____

_____

_____

_____

Boundaries and Spirituality

Having your boundaries ruptured in a shock trauma can occasionally result in a sweeping experience of the transcendent. It is possible, that as your body constricts and contracts with a traumatic impact, your awareness, hurled though your energetic boundaries, experiences a profound expansive state. Traumatic ruptured boundaries are capable of providing the possibility of the transformation of consciousness, due to the encounter with what lies on the other side of the boundary. However, you are at risk of remaining in a disembodied state, meant to protect you from terrifying shock and pain. The trauma effects can remain unresolved, hidden deeply in your body's memory.

Yet even if you feel, as you reconnect with the buried pain from your trauma, that these profound experiences of interconnectedness and unity have vanished and are inaccessible, you will gain access again over time. In fact, your spiritual connection may deepen once you resolve your trauma.

WHAT I LEARNED IN THIS CHAPTER

Spend a few minutes reflecting on this chapter and record what was most relevant for you.

_____

_____

_____

_____

_____

_____

CHAPTER 8

Working with Shame

Shame is an awful emotion that can block the experience of connection and the feeling of love. Toxic shame brings a sense of badness and constriction that disrupts your joy and aliveness. Shame brings feelings of unworthiness and low self-esteem, but the sense of "I'm bad" is especially excruciating. For who can believe they are loved for who they are when they consciously or unconsciously feel they are *bad*?

Shame may emerge in adulthood as your interpretation of the distress from early trauma. Rather than feeling shame for something that you did, or perceived you did wrong in response to your caregiver's reaction, you allocate shame to who you are. *It feels bad: therefore, I'm bad.* This becomes toxic shame.

How you identify yourself as a child is determined by your environment. It's very difficult as a child to experience your inherent goodness in what feels like a bad situation. You see yourself as the cause of the difficulties around you, unless you have a very conscious primary caregiver who is aware and takes precautionary measures so you know you are goodness and love in challenging situations.

Shame doesn't feel good, yet it serves an important purpose. In a *good enough environment* as a child, shame has a positive learning curve that serves you. The feeling of shame signals something is *wrong*. Shame, especially when you're a child, allows you to understand boundaries: what is socially acceptable and what is not. Shame will also prevent you from repeating mistakes, making you safer.

Toxic shame begins in the early years of life with the loss of contact with the love and nurturance of your parent. This is how it *feels* to you, not what may be true. Long before there could even be any wrongdoing on your part, you can *feel* wrong, bad, and unlovable when the experience of shame embeds within you. Fortunately, you can dissolve that experience from your body, diminish the erroneous beliefs that go with it, and reawaken the deeply loving contact with your being.

Shame can emerge when an acute trauma immobilizes us, often as the first feeling of that freeze response. You can dissipate this shame as you recognize and acknowledge that immobility is nonvolitional; that your system was simply trying to survive.

When you're healing trauma, shame can be challenging. Yet you can compassionately understand, harness, and transform this energy, further illuminating your inherent wisdom and spirituality—and regain the deep connection you've longed for.

In this chapter you'll explore the deeper underpinnings of shame. You'll learn ways to compassionately and effectively work with shame to reduce its negative effects and release its grip, and you'll focus on its powerful transformative properties.

When shame is triggered, you're highly sensitive and your cognition is impaired. If you bring shame into your awareness too soon it can overwhelm you. If you notice this, slow down, ground yourself, and try some supportive practices; for instance:

- Evoke the quality or attributes of compassion; this helps diminish the experience of shame.

- Be sensitive to your needs; for example, *I need holding; I need to feel that I'm okay.* Giving yourself *now* that which may have been missing at the time of a trauma can be extremely powerful and soothing.

- If you experience self-criticism, acknowledge an angry part of you is trying to protect you. Offer it compassion and gratitude. By not rejecting a part of your consciousness that once was rejected or disconnected, you aid integration. Offer words such as *You experienced some painful times; it was never your fault; you did nothing wrong; you didn't receive the support you needed; you're not bad—you are love.*

- Pause and feel your body. How does it feel to be more compassionate toward your inner experience?

_____

_____

- Learning that shame can be resolved and no longer a part of your inner experience, how do you feel? A sense of relief or hope—or maybe some fear, as shame is so challenging to confront?

  _____

  _____

- Describe any positive or less difficult experiences in this learning so far. Does it still feel frightening to touch this emotion?

  _____

  _____

As you begin exploring shame, know that you don't *have* to address it directly. You may decide to, depending on where you are on your healing path and what feels right for you, and what unfolds.

By reconnecting to your body and enhancing body awareness, you'll feel more of the natural and innate impulses and emotions that once seemed like too much. There are many aspects to shame. You may have unconsciously *chosen* shame over anger, because aggression can feel so overwhelmingly awful—the intensity of feeling rage can be terrifying. Shame can cover the feelings of anger and aggression that you once pushed down or dissociated. With the work you've done so far, you may be beginning to feel, observe, and set those emotions free. As you gently tap into and then embody the experiences of aggression, your physiology begins to shift, and with awareness and a new sense of internal power and agency, shame can naturally dissolve. This is the beauty of body awareness: it can illuminate what you don't see directly and liberate it, without directly addressing it.

When shame feels intolerable, you'll do anything to avoid feeling it. You may want to disappear, hide, run away, attack others, project your shame onto them, withdraw, shut down, or collapse. Your unconscious strategies against feeling this emotion can arise so instantaneously that it's difficult to distinguish them from other strategies or adaptive responses.

THE POSTURE OF SHAME

The experience and sensations of toxic shame often create a compromised posture: a curled spine, rounded shoulders, a lowering of your head, and avoidance of eye contact with others, often with a horrible feeling in the pit of your stomach. Some individuals may overcompensate for their shame by taking on a more prideful identity, so the posture of shame isn't evident. Instead of caving in, a person may have an energetically armored chest, appearing to thrust forward. Both postures indicate inner shame.

- Notice how you're sitting right now. How would you describe your shoulders? Soft, hunched, rounded, relaxed?

  _____

- How would you describe your spine? Rounded, straight, collapsed, upright?

  _____

- How would you describe the front of your torso, especially your chest area? Open, closed, collapsed, guarded?

  _____

- Is your chest area inflated? (This can cover up feelings of helplessness and vulnerability.)   **Yes   No**

- How would you describe your overall posture? For instance, collapsed, hunched, closed, upright, rigid, relaxed, open, a mix of tension and flaccidity?

  _____

- Do you ever feel like you try to make yourself smaller or less visible?   **Yes   No**

- If so, what feelings make you want to do so? For example, feeling shy, unlovable, unworthy, lacking self-esteem, embarrassed?

  _____

- Can you describe the sensations you feel when you experience shame? For example, a sinking stomach, nausea, constriction in the chest, dread?

  _____

- Describe how you feel exploring your posture and experience of shame.

  _____

  _____

  _____

Being aware of how shame lives in and affects your body is essential to resolving it. The next exercise will help you become more aware of your experience of shame and support you in moving through it with greater awareness. The first part is designed to slightly rouse your experience of shame—the posture and feelings associated with it—while helping you not identify with or be consumed by it. As you do this exercise, be curious about the following:

- Sensations

- Emotions

- Feelings

- Thoughts

- Insights

- Perceptions

Your curiosity and body awareness are great allies in keeping your executive functioning online and present as you open your awareness. If something particularly salient occurs, pause and deepen your curiosity.

Your observation skills, openness, and curiosity allow you to notice thoughts and impressions, letting them come and go without grasping them. This approach will help you continue to cultivate your sense of presence, allowing you to observe your inner experiences with greater depth and clarity. Remaining relaxed while your mind is alert (not vigilant) is a good indicator of your deepening presence and the unfolding of your inherent wisdom.

Your underlying assumptions strongly influence your state of mind and behavior.[59] Challenging your assumptions elicits your sense of agency. For instance, if you find yourself in a place or posture in which you feel safe—say, if you're curled up and hiding—ask yourself, *Is this really safe now? Or is this my early consciousness feeling safe by hiding?*

EXERCISE: Unfurling Shame into Dignity

You may carry shame within you, never thinking to purposely unfurl yourself from it. This gentle exercise can give you the experience of coming out of the feeling and posture of shame. The new feeling can be exhilarating. You may also feel some emotion such as sadness. See whether, whatever arises, you can simply be with it.

Before you begin, read the exercise. (An audio recording of instructions for this exercise is available at http://www.newharbinger.com/43256.) As you work with shame in this way, if anything feels like it's *too much*, pause and slow down, or come back to the exercise at another time. You'll be following your movement very slowly using micromovements. Notice whether you hold your breath, and remember to keep breathing! You can try this exercise a few times in one sitting.

1. Begin by sitting on a chair. Sometimes it helps to have a pillow on your lap; the pillow will support you if you move into a deep curled or collapsed posture.

2. Feel into any of the shame-based aspects of your posture—rounded shoulders, curled spine, lowered head, avoidant gaze, collapsed chest. Notice any sensations and emotions.

3. Begin to exaggerate your shame-based posture by *very slowly* rounding your spine and feeling a collapse in your chest. Allow the front of your torso to constrict, your head lowering, your shoulders hunching and rounding. Stay curious; be aware and observe how your body feels, noticing any emotions, images, and perceptions.

4. When something feels particularly potent or poignant, pause and notice how you feel. Get curious. Ask *What is here?* There may be images, thoughts, perceptions, emotions, memories, and so on. When you're ready, continue into a deeper posture that represents shame.

5. Pause your movement when you've connected with a sense of inner shame. Ask yourself some questions:

    •   What is it like to be in this posture?

    _____

    _____

    •   How does shame feel?

    _____

    _____

    •   Is your experience of shame familiar or unfamiliar?

    _____

    _____

    •   Is this posture comfortable or uncomfortable, painful or pleasant?

    _____

    •   Do you have a sense of being younger as you pause in this posture? If so, observe that sense from your adult perspective.

6. Begin to very slowly unfurl from this posture. Keep a keen sense of how your body feels.

7. As you *slowly* roll up and your posture opens, notice everything you can in your body.

8. Roll all the way up until you're upright—your chin is level, your shoulders are back, your chest is open. You may spontaneously take a deep breath. Notice how this breath feels as you remain open and curious for a few moments.

9. Stay with any positive feelings and sensations for at least thirty seconds.

10. Now, as you sit upright, look around you. See the world from this open posture. Notice how you feel inside, and how your environment looks to you now.

- What feels different?

- Do you notice any softening in your body?

- Do you notice life force moving in your body now that you've come out of the collapse and constriction of shame?

11. Try saying a phrase or two in this upright posture; for example:

- I'm safe, I'm confident.

- I'm love. I love. I'm open.

- I survived. I'm okay now. I survived.

12. Describe your experience, especially positive or empowering feelings.

_____

_____

_____

As you continue to do this exercise, your body may feel like it's growing bigger. This is the life force moving in your physical and subtle body—a very positive indicator of healing. Remain present and aware of your life force moving and an embodied spiritual connection returning you to your true self.

EXERCISE: How I Shame Myself

The following statements express very deep, painful experiences of suffering—which can emerge from any form of trauma—that you may have hidden from yourself or tried to avoid. You may recognize that you shame yourself for these actions. Many statements arise from self-loathing, and compassion is always an antidote. Underline any that apply to you.

- I feel powerless and helpless and try to hide these experiences.

- I feel inadequate. I feel like I don't fit in.

- Sometimes I feel shame at existing. (*This is a profound statement; please remain aware of your response. If you're tapping into this, take the necessary steps to feel safe, grounded, and connected.*)

- I feel like I'm a burden on others.

- I feel flawed, unworthy of love.

- I feel rejected and so deeply shamed about this.

- I feel shame at having needs. I try not show I have needs.

As you look over the experiences you underlined, what is your experience? Is there any relief in the acknowledgment of your experience, knowing that these are common examples? Describe this.

_____

_____

Replace any negative statements with a positive statement and notice how you feel as you express out loud and write it down. You are creating another option. For instance, if you underlined *I feel flawed and unworthy of love*, try *I am a success exactly as I am in this moment; I am love* or *I embrace and accept myself, I am love and I am loved*. To paraphrase Shakespeare: our destiny is not in the stars but in ourselves. You are not tied to the fate of your trauma; you are, at least in part, the creator of your own destiny.

_____

_____

_____

_____

_____

THE CHILDHOOD WOUND OF SHAME

The relationship of your caregivers with you is an inextricable part of your developing sense of self and whether you can remain connected to your most authentic expression. You learn what is acceptable and unacceptable to your caregivers and develop concepts of who you are based on what you feel your caregivers expect, need, or want from you.[60] Your caregivers' inability to attune to you well or acknowledge you, or their disapproval of you may have created profound (conscious or unconscious) internal feelings of lack of self-esteem, self-worth, badness. These are shame-based feelings.

THE EMERGENCE OF SHAME

There are many reasons you may feel shame as a child. The point is not to remember them, but to uproot the embedded experience of shame that you may still be carrying. However, it's useful to understand how shame can become toxic.

Imagine, as a child, as you joyously and spontaneously explore your environment, you see a shiny object. You innocently reach up to touch it. Your mother sees you're about to pull down a large lamp. She screams "No! Don't touch that!" Her eyes look angry or scared; she rushes to pull you away. It must be *you* who has upset your mom; *you're* bad. Your body fills with a most uncomfortable sensation, which you'll come to know as shame. Your mother places you someplace she considers safe in the room and goes about her business. Her angry or annoyed eyes may have felt punitive or demeaning, a shock and humiliation in your undefended state. The shame it causes can stay within you if not followed by a smile or other reassurance that you're okay—you're not *bad*.

You mother simply did not think to tell you that:

- You're okay; she is keeping you safe.

- You did nothing wrong.

- She loves you.

By doing so, she would *repair* this small rupture in your relationship; you know it's okay to be *you*, and the shame quickly dissolves and doesn't become embedded within you. You learn to not touch the lamp, and the world is again safe to explore openly.

Your caregiver's reaction keeps you safe. It can alert you to danger, issue warnings that stop you in your tracks. This eye contact is crucial for communication and also a primary mechanism for healthy brain organization and growth in your early life.

When such incidents happen repeatedly, without repair, shame becomes chronic and toxic. You internalize your caregiver's reactions in ways that significantly affect how you see yourself and the world. You may determine at that early age that it's not safe to be spontaneous, open, vulnerable—to be *you*. You may close your capacity for vulnerability or spontaneity, stuffing them into your unconscious, where they await your rediscovery.

As shame can feel so crushing, knowing your habitual response to it is fundamental to your healing. When you're aware of moving away from shame, you can begin to gently face and transform it.

When you experience shame, are you aware of doing any of the following behaviors to avoid feeling it? Underline any that apply.

- Withdrawing

- Dissociating

- Attacking/shaming others

- Having self-sabotaging thoughts

- Becoming overly prideful

- Using avoidant behavior to avoid your inner experience in some way

- Are there other ways you avoid shame feeling?

  _____

  _____

- Describe how it feels to acknowledge your patterns around shame.

  _____

  _____

- Write out other, healthier ways you can now face or address feelings of shame, including the exercises in this or other chapters.

  _____

  _____

  _____

  _____

SHAME AND IMMOBILITY

Shame can come from an immobility response in which you felt shame about not being able to defend yourself. When Frank was held up with a knife, he experienced deep shame as he froze and couldn't defend himself. He judged himself terribly, damning himself for not fighting back. He described his shame as a sinking pool of darkness in his stomach. When he learned that his freeze response was out of his control, the grip of shame loosened. If you've experienced immobility in a traumatic event like an assault, rape, or combat, understanding that immobility is an involuntary reflex may begin to relieve your shame and guilt.

PAUSE FOR REFLECTION

Do you recall a traumatic experience in which you froze? Knowing what you know now, what would you tell yourself? Spend a few minutes writing compassionately to yourself, letting yourself know it was not your fault. Feel your body, as you bring forth the quality of compassion and any other resources and positive qualities that you have now.

_____

_____

_____

_____

_____

YOUR BODY AND AWARENESS

You're likely more connected to your experience now than when you began this healing journey. You have many more resources and tools to feel secure and safe as you become aware of things that have been too uncomfortable and painful to face. Shame can be a catastrophic whole-body experience leading to varying degrees of disconnection. Shame cannot be banished or resolved with understanding and words alone; it must be accepted as part of your human experience, resolved with your transfiguring posture, bathed in compassion, and met with deepening awareness and presence.

Becoming aware of your internal experience is crucial for your healing and growth. Your mind's content is not always obvious. Developing your metacognitive skills helps with this. Metacognition is the direct perception of your own state of mind or another's, including both cognitive and emotional experience.[61] Deepening your metacognitive skills can be as simple as noticing what you're feeling in the moment.

- What are you feeling right now? The more you focus, the more specific the feeling will become.

_____

_____

_____

_____

- As your feelings become clearer, write the words that best describe them.

_____

_____

_____

_____

A COMPASSIONATE EMBRACE

Shame heals when it's held in compassion—when you feel attuned to, accepted and loved. You're cultivating this sacred relationship with yourself. As you tend to yourself, you're giving yourself what others may not have been able to give you and fulfilling the needs they may not have been able to. You're holding yourself in a way that you weren't after an acute trauma. You're understanding the suffering you may have endured. You're empowering yourself and building greater self-agency and deep spiritual connection. In the next exercise, imagining a compassionate being holding you elicits inner compassion, helping dispel negative feelings, emotions, and beliefs you may still have about yourself.

EXERCISE: A Compassionate Embrace

In this exercise, for simplicity's sake I use the pronoun *she* for the being you envision. (An audio recording of instructions for this exercise is available at http://www.newharbinger.com/43256.)

1. Sitting comfortably, take a few deep breaths. On each exhale, let go of any tension and feel your body relax more deeply.

2. Bring your awareness to this moment. Sitting in presence, bring to mind your compassionate being, a source of infinite compassion.

3. Imagine this being sitting about three feet in front of you. Visualize the being with as much sensual detail as possible. Take your time. See her sparkling eyes exuding love toward you. She knows everything about you—your pain, your shame, your trauma—and she loves you unconditionally. She understands the nature of all suffering. Feel the compassion emanating from her; see it as light moving from her heart into yours. Stay present with the image for a few moments.

4. Feel her loving warmth like sunlight filling the space around you. Place all your worries, anxieties, fears, and doubts in this field of love and acceptance. Watch them dissolve in this unconditional love. Release all limiting beliefs that keep you from your fullest potential into this love with a simple intention to do so. Like clouds, they dissolve in the brilliant light. Feel her support your healing. Her smile and compassion are a gentle nudge to wake you up from pain and suffering. Surrender your feelings of unworthiness and worthlessness and being *bad*. Watch them dissolve in her radiant love. Take in the love that streams from her eyes.

5. Now imagine she turns into a golden sphere of light. See the light move toward your heart center, where it enters. Feel the golden sphere of compassion pulsing within you.

6. The sphere begins to expand, radiating through your entire body. You're connecting with and filling yourself from the source of compassion. Let this quality sink deeply into every cell of your being.

7. From this place of radiating inner compassion, allow and invite any images, memories, or thoughts of yourself being in shame to come into awareness. Embrace those images, memories, and thoughts in your body of compassion. Feel the shame dissolving in the light of compassion. Stay with this as long as you are able.

8. Allow the compassion that radiates through your whole body to return to the sphere of light and into your heart center. Now move it into your heart organ, where it will remain, accessible at any time.

When you're ready to return, slowly open your eyes and look around. Notice your experience of yourself now. Spend a few moments being still and feeling your body. Take three deep breaths to transition out of the practice before you describe your experience here.

_____

_____

_____

_____

_____

_____

_____

_____

TERROR OF ANNIHILATION

I work with many individuals who, when they touch into shame and other intense emotions, simultaneously touch a terrifying sense of approaching doom. This is closely linked with the terror of annihilation common in trauma and trauma healing—a horrifying sense of *existing in nonexistence*! Touching into annihilation with awareness can lead to knowing what is indestructible within you—a deep spiritual experience. When you touch a fear of death you find a kernel of life, a spiritual awakening and maturation born through transforming suffering.

Take a moment to reflect on approaching the terror of annihilation:

- Pause and notice your experience.

- If you feel unsettled, as this subject can be at the very core of trauma, return to any of the earlier stabilizing exercises. If you're curious about your experience right now and feel grounded enough, continue.

- Any frightening emotion—but especially shame, anger, and rage—can evoke the terror of annihilation. Know that your organism once felt this impending sense of doom—which often happens with immobility or shutdown. Right now *you're okay*. You have many resources to keep you feeling connected and in the *here and now*.

- Touching into the terror of annihilation is often best explored with a therapist. Don't go beyond what you feel you can alone. I'm simply sharing the depth of what often lies at the core of trauma healing and its spiritual potential.

- This is best explored with another person and practiced only when you have developed a sense of being embodied and can remain connected to your body.

- Gently touching the fear of annihilation with your awareness can disempower the experience and empower you. But you must remain present, grounded.

- If you are aware of the feeling of annihilation or existing in nonexistence, touch it very lightly with your awareness, remaining rooted in your body, then reorient yourself in the present.

- Describe your experience.

- Repeat the exercise if it felt helpful.

ANNIHILATION AND THE IMMOBILITY RESPONSE

The immobility response, explored in earlier chapters, prepared you to shut down in case death might ensue. It didn't, but part of your consciousness that split off does not know this. It remains in an in-between state, at the age you were then. You may experience the terror you touch into through the lens of your infant or child consciousness. So it's crucial to develop your sense of agency and your capacity to stay observant in the present moment.

- What do you notice right now? Has your breathing changed in any way?   **Yes**   **No**

- Did the words about annihilation and existence/nonexistence touch you in any way?   **Yes**   **No**

- Are you experiencing any form of fear, even in a subtle way?   **Yes**   **No**

- Take care of yourself: ground, connect, move your body. Your repertoire of resources and skills is widening; use them consistently.

- Try repeating "I survived." Pause and feel your body. If this feels like it may be too much, try later when you are more resourced and embodied.

At first, the transformation you are creating through these exercises and visualizations may feel elusive or subtle. It will gain momentum and strength as you gradually leave these familiar, destructive feelings and patterns behind you and embody the love and compassion that you are.

WHAT I LEARNED IN THIS CHAPTER

Describe any insights and body awareness that have emerged through this chapter. And remember, healing is nonlinear, progressing over time. You may return to many of the exercises and find a deeper layer of healing each time.

_____

_____

_____

_____

_____

_____

_____

CHAPTER 9

Imagine Your Trauma Differently

Your imagination is a great resource, a gentle ally, and a powerful influence on your healing journey. In this chapter you'll learn some colorful visualization and imaginative techniques.

Imagination is much more than mere fantasy; its aesthetic quality can be central to your experience. Your imagination is not solely visual; you may be able to see, hear, smell, feel, and taste what emerges from your imaginings. When you allow yourself to fully experience your responses to the exercises, they become more than something you're just making up. Visualizations, intentions, and conscious use of imagery have been shown to play a considerable role in positive outcomes in the treatment of physical injuries, illness, and trauma.[62]

In this chapter you're invited to cultivate corrective experiences that override old painful memories and fill your body/mind with new, more positive ones. You can't change the past, but it need no longer upset your present. As image and imagination flow through your brain and body, they help you create a transformed story, moving through trauma into resilience, joy, greater freedom, and the realization of your authentic, heartfelt being.

The following exercise helps with your body's coherence, focusing on your organs. Your body has an inherent ability to function effectively as a whole. But a traumatized body often feels like it's fragmented; you look connected but don't feel that way. In a state of *coherence*, your body is self-regulating and self-organizing. Your heart rate, organs, vascular system, respiratory rate, and micromuscular activity enter a more harmonious and balanced state, and your innate wisdom and self-healing capacity functions more effectively and efficiently.

EXERCISE: Creating Somatic Coherence

Imagine a symbol—a sphere of light—to represent the highest level of consciousness you know. This could symbolize God, spirit, consciousness beyond your subjective self, the mystery of the universe or cosmos, or unconditional love. Traditional Chinese medicine tells us that particular emotions such as anger, fear, nervous tension, and worry are each associated with a particular organ; for example, the kidneys with fear. Focusing the sphere of light (your awareness) on a particular organ can bring connection and coherence to the organ and its related structures. This can also facilitate a gentle energetic release of the emotion that may be bound within the organ. This meditative exercise also calms the ANS (which innervates your organs), so you can experience yourself at ease, present, and strong. To allow full immersion in the exercise, you could have a friend read the exercise to you or record it yourself. (You can also listen to my recording at http://www.newharbinger.com/43256.)

1. Sit in a comfortable upright position.

2. Take three deep breaths. With each exhale, feel your body soften, releasing tension.

3. Bring your awareness to the center of your chest—your heart center. Begin by imagining a sphere of brilliant, radiant light here, golden white or the color of your choice. This light should represent the highest consciousness you can imagine or pure unconditional love. Imagine you can feel it radiating with love in your heart center.

4. Now, from the sphere of light in your chest, another sphere of light emerges. This light moves into your heart organ, filling it with radiant light and evoking awakened consciousness of the heart organ. The heart begins to vibrate at its healthiest frequency—its awakened essence. Feel (or, an option with each step of this exercise, *imagine* you can feel) your heart pulsing and vibrating with this essence and light. Stay with this for a minute. Imagine any traumatic energy being released from your heart; any anxiety, depression, and restlessness easily flows outward and leaves your body, as the light from the sphere radiates throughout your heart. Imagine joy filling your heart as we are working with your heart organ.

5. Return your attention to the sphere of light at your heart center. Two smaller spheres of light emerge from your heart center and move into your kidneys and the attached adrenals. Feel these organs gently vibrating as they fill with light and the essence of the light resonates with their awakened consciousness. Ancestral and intergenerational

trauma and fear flow out of your kidneys; exhaustion flows out of the adrenals. Feel these organs becoming brighter, filling with their awakened essence. You feel increasingly calm and fearless as your past is released. Rest and feel the radiance in your kidneys and adrenals for a minute.

6.   Return to your heart center sphere. Two spheres of light emerge from its center and move into your lungs. Feel your lungs vibrating as the light fills them. Sadness, grief, and uncontrollable crying flow out of your lungs, and they vibrate with radiant loving light. Feel the vibration of their awakened essence and the quality of courage. Rest here, feeling the radiance and vibrancy in your lungs for a minute.

7.   Return to your heart center sphere. Another sphere of light emerges and moves into your liver. Feel your liver vibrating softly as it's filled with light and its consciousness is awakened. Unresolved anger, resentment, irritability, and frustration are released and dissolve in the glow. The quality of kindness fills your liver. Rest here, feeling the radiance and vibrancy in your liver for a few moments.

8.   Return to your heart center sphere. Another sphere of light emerges and moves into your spleen. Feel your spleen vibrating with radiant light. Worry and overthinking flow out of your spleen and dissolve. Imagine your spleen vibrating with sweetness and fairness as it fills with light and its essence. Rest here, feeling the sweetness awakened in your spleen.

9.   Return to your heart center sphere. Another sphere of light emerges and moves into your stomach and pancreas. Feel them beginning to glow and gently vibrate in this radiant light and their awakened essence. Feel any undigested emotions leaving. Feel a deep quality of equanimity in your stomach and pancreas. Rest for a minute in the overflowing essence of equanimity.

10. Return to your heart center sphere. Now imagine this sphere of light begins to expand outward until it encircles your whole body. Allow your body to rest in this glowing light for a minute, simply feeling a soft vibratory quality of peace and radiance as your body becomes a field of gently vibrating light of love.

11. Take a deep breath as you let the imagery dissipate. Notice how your body and mind feel.

12. Observe for a few moments. Then, as you continue to observe, write about your experience, staying connected to the felt sense of your body.

_____

_____

_____

_____

_____

_____

Part of your work is to find and integrate—transcending through inclusion—any early traumatized consciousness that may have split off and become frozen or encapsulated in time. Fortunately, you don't have to remember every traumatizing event. An organic process of reorganization and integration will naturally occur. You're hardwired to heal. Creating safe and nurturing conditions through these exercises, you're enhancing this process.

Perhaps suffering that is transcended is worthwhile. Transcendence does not mean leaving anything behind; it's bringing into wholeness all those parts of yourselves that you lost, rejected, or denied—parts you closed yourself off from and hid away.

I imagine we all have these encapsulated child states, frozen in time, waiting for us to retrieve them and move them forward to foster emotional maturity and psychospiritual growth. As you continue with the exercises, you'll find that you feel more alive and more of your life force is available for your creative expression.

Although you may want to forget many of the traumatic imprints of your past, they sometimes (though not always or necessarily) need to be remembered at some level for healing. When you remember intentionally in the right conditions, it can be a healing opportunity, and you'll be better able to harness the energies for integration, whatever form they're in—emotions, memories, sensations, or thoughts.

YOUR AUTHENTIC QUALITIES OF BEING

Next comes a reconnaissance of your authentic self. You'll explore, through your imagination, a way to reclaim authentic qualities of your being that you may have hidden deep in your unconscious.

The unresolved feelings, emotions, and memories that lie dormant in your unconscious can emerge and flow into your consciousness at any time. Your unresolved past frequently washes up on the shores of your conscious mind, influencing you. Even if you're unaware of this, you're still affected. Sometimes the waves are gentle; other times they feel like a tsunami, flooding you with intrusive thoughts and frightening emotions.

In the past, you've done your best, when you could, to avoid overwhelming experiences by not feeling them or pushing them away. Or if what emerged was too painful and overwhelming, you may have been devastated and dropped into despair or depression, or experienced bouts of anguish and anger. But you've now learned so much, including mastering several exercises, that you're likely able to feel more in your body and better self-regulate. You have new ways of being with your trauma; it's no longer so overwhelming. Now you may be ready to experience more, to push your tolerance boundaries.

Do you feel you can tolerate more energy, emotion, sensation, feelings in your body than when you began this workbook? This doesn't necessarily mean you feel *better*; it means tolerating more without becoming overwhelmed—a good sign that you're healing. The work you're doing can be quite subtle; you may not even recognize your expanding capacity for feeling different elements of your being. In this next exercise, you'll reflect on your physical experience and different life situations.

EXERCISE: Your Feeling Experience

• The places in my body where I'm beginning to feel more are: [for example, my upper chest, my stomach when I relax, my legs, all over my body]

_____

_____

_____

- The pleasant sensations and emotions I notice are: [for example, excitement, calmness, tingling, happiness]. Include *where* in your body you notice these.

  _____

  _____

  _____

- The unpleasant sensations and emotions I notice more of are: [for example, anxiety, sadness, grief]. Include *where*.

  _____

  _____

  _____

- I notice I feel more sensations and emotions in the following situations: [for example, practicing breathing techniques, with my friends, at work, when talking about certain topics, on waking in the morning, when doing the workbook exercises]

  _____

  _____

  _____

- My overall experience of feeling more energy, emotion, and sensation is

  _____

  _____

  _____

YOUR AUTHENTIC SELF

Evolution designed our human brains, minds, and bodies to be open and receptive, to grow in response to one another and the environment. Humans are inherently social beings. Your nervous system illustrates this. This is not always recognized, especially by caregivers when we are young. I see the failures of caregivers not as *not caring* but as *not knowing*—an inability to attend to your needs because of their own past and present adverse experiences. When your caregivers are attuned to you—when they beam with pleasure when seeing you, smile at your successes, and resonate empathically with your distress—you naturally learn to be *okay* with your developing being. Your sense of self and your inner world—your subjective experience— develop from and are fostered by this relationship and shape how you interact with others.

When your caregivers couldn't nurture the growth of your authentic self, you adapted by cutting yourself off from it—an instinctual way to survive what feels frightening. Now, through the exercises here you identify and reclaim feeling states and qualities once perceived as unsafe, you reembody them. You're disengaging from adaptations and patterns of survival that don't serve you anymore.

EXERCISE: Part 1, Reclaiming Your Authentic Self

You can do these two parts together or separately. You'll explore your depth of authenticity to foster strength and greater awareness, helping you dissolve survival patterns and allow repressed qualities back into your awareness and sense of being. (An audio recording of instructions for this exercise is available at http://www.newharbinger.com/43256.)

The images or symbols you evoke don't have to be tangible; they can be shapes, empty space, colors, or objects. Try not to *go into your head* wondering what the symbols mean. An insight will likely come later even if what you see isn't clearly recognizable.

1. Sit comfortably and relax into a receptive state. Silently set an intention: *I'm encountering and embodying the authentic qualities of my being.*

2. Imagine that in your home you see a door. Notice the crystal doorknob. Curious, you open the door and enter. You start climbing stairs toward an attic. There is just enough light in the attic to see a large wooden chest against the far wall. You walk to it and open the heavy lid. Inside you feel a fairly large wooden box. Bring it out; you see your name on the lid with the words "authentic quality of being." Open the lid and notice inside the first image or symbol that comes to your mind. As you look at it, notice any

body sensations or emotions. Spend a few moments in relationship with the symbol as you hold the box. Now place the open box on a table next to the chest.

3. Reach into the chest for another box with the same message. As you open it, notice the first thing you see: symbol, image, color, or something else. Notice your body sensations and emotions. Spend a few moments with this symbol and what you feel. Place the open box on the table by the other box.

4. Reach into the chest for another box. Open the box and notice what you see. Spend a few moments with whatever you see, being aware of your body. Place the open box on the table.

5. Take one more box from the chest. As you open it and see what it holds, be aware of what you're experiencing in your body. After a few moments, place the open box with the others and take a step back.

6. Simply observe the symbols and images and notice how you feel. Imagine you can breathe these qualities into your body or mind, or place them around you, or feel them deep inside you. Connect with them so that you're embodying as much as you can, so you feel them within you or *as you*.

7. When you're ready, go back down the stairs. Notice that you feel different—maybe stronger, more confident. Know you can return any time and revisit the chest to find more qualities of your being that may have become disconnected from your embodied way of being in the world.

Record your qualities of being from the imagined boxes.

Box 1	Box 2	Box 3	Box 4

Now describe your experience, including sensations, emotions, perceptions, thoughts, and feelings.

_____

_____

_____

_____

_____

_____

As you continue with the workbook, stay connected to your qualities. Remind yourself to feel them, to encode them within you as you embody them. Enjoy the fruits of your practices by remembering and feeling.

In trauma, so many aspects of your consciousness can become frozen, stuck in terrorized paralysis in your unconscious, rendering you unable to realize your full potential. You may be very aware of some of your trauma but still unable to quite connect it to your current experiences or symptoms. Or you may not be able to come out of being stuck in some areas of your life and get back into the flow of life. For many people, visualization can tenderly penetrate the paralyzed parts of their consciousness, sending colorful vitality to the parts caught in the impact of trauma. Gently using your imagination allows you to integrate those isolated, frozen parts and heal.

In Part 2 of this exercise, you go back to the past and tend to the child aspect of your consciousness that may be frozen in time.

EXERCISE: Part 2, Integrating Early Consciousness

This exercise helps you be as connected as possible, reintegrating with the qualities you discovered in part 1 and beginning from this place of strength and confidence (or other new feelings). You're bringing in a corrective experience to override the old fearful one. Your adult consciousness will speak to and hold the child consciousness, with reassurance that you're bringing what was missing at the time of the trauma. You could say the threat is now over, that the child is not alone, and safety is here now. If you aren't visual, use any other sense that is available for you. (An audio recording of instructions for this exercise is available at http://www.newharbinger.com/43256.)

1. Begin by tuning into and feeling your qualities and symbols from part 1 as deeply as you can in your body. Spend a few moments really connecting to them as a felt sense.

2. Now choose one of your qualities or symbols to work with in this exercise.

3. Remember a time when you were young, when this authentic way of being may have been discounted and disconnected. You don't have to remember a real story; memory is fluid and changing. You may have what feels like a memory, or you may imagine, given what you know about your childhood and caregiver, what may have happened to disconnect you from this quality or authentic way of being.

4. As you remember, tune into that aspect of yourself, the child in that memory. Notice the feeling tone of that child: were you sad, fearful, angry, in shock, withdrawn?

5. Attune to your child consciousness. Notice what the child needs—to be seen, heard, held, observed, gently soothed? Gently begin to address these needs and continue to be with the child in whatever way is needed.

6. When it feels right, bring the child into your heart center. You may need to revisit this memory a few times before you can do this. It's most important that you attune and respond to what you feel that child part of you needs.

Now describe your experience with parts 1 and 2. Describe your feelings, emotions, and sensations, and how you feel now compared to when you began the exercises.

_____

_____

_____

_____

_____

NATURAL RESPONSES TO GROWTH

As self-awareness of your mental and emotional states grows, it becomes easier to recognize and release the identities and patterns you've adopted, including those you once felt you needed for survival. As you may have noticed, it doesn't always feel good to dismantle patterns that once served to protect you, but now they limit you. As you release patterns, you may feel chaos and confusion—it's as if the pattern is desperately trying to hold on, to stay. Patterns usually do not go gracefully. Grief also indicates that a pattern is dying, as does fear—often it's fear of the unknown. Sadness may surface too. If you notice any of these, it's vital to stay as present as you can with the emotions. Grief, especially, allows you to release the past of what could have been so something new and fresh can emerge.

Being aware of these responses to change will allow you to stay more present as positive change happens, rather than getting caught up in the emotion. For many, the *last stand* of the pattern comes after a period of feeling good, so the upsurge of emotion feels like a step backward. Don't be fooled: it's the pattern trying to reestablish itself one last time. Stay present. When the energy of your awareness is greater than the energy of the pattern, it's easier to pull the energy of the pattern into your awareness. As a pattern releases, the energy goes somewhere; if not to your awareness, then it may reestablish itself in the old pattern. That pattern may seem to be gone for a while yet later manifest in a different way, becoming more resilient. However, with all the self-observation skills you're learning, the energy will flow into your awareness, strengthening that perspective and expanding your consciousness.

WHAT I LEARNED IN THIS CHAPTER

Write about your overall experience of this chapter and what felt relevant for your healing.

_____

_____

_____

_____

_____

_____

_____

CHAPTER 10

Using Anger to Transform Your Consciousness

Life is beautiful, painful, filled with love and joy and loss and grief; it's melancholic and cheerful; it's bittersweet, marvelous, and calamitous; and through it all, life can be filled with delightful expressions of being. To know and feel all the wonders of the human experience, you need to resolve unresolved anger in your body while you're present and aware. When you resolve anger and reweave it as life force back into your body, you become internally powerful, reconnecting with your intuition, vitality, and inherent wisdom.

As you return fully to your body, you'll feel sensations of intense anger, even rage, as these emotions underlie many trauma responses. To transform anger, you must first have an authentic connection with your body and a comfort in feeling the flow of your life force energy. Then you can remain connected to experience and stay present with this potentially volatile emotion, disengaging if you begin to feel too much.

Anger arises from feelings of helplessness and powerlessness, from having your desires and needs denied and your boundaries violated. Unresolved anger upsets your mood, increases body tensions, and drains your energy. As you resolve anger or rage, you'll soften and be energized, and your heart will open to love.

Anger, like trauma, is dual natured. In its negative form, you express it by lashing out at others, creating harm, distress, and upset; when it has been suppressed or dissociated, it can turn back on you in the form of self-loathing, self-hatred, and self-criticism. You're unconsciously subject to its frequently negative influence. You may continue to try and repress your anger, but it will continue to disrupt your inner world until it's resolved. You may project your anger onto others, seeing it as *out there* rather than within. You may even use anger to avoid your awareness of more vulnerable states like shame. When you live with unresolved anger, parts of you may remain primed for danger. In this state, it's not always easy to distinguish others' real intentions. You may become very defensive even when someone is trying to help you. Or you may remain feeling helpless and powerless, disconnected from your vitality and internal strength.

In its healthy form, anger is an emotion derived from the SNS, geared to energize you to set boundaries and fend off danger. Anger informs you when danger approaches, when your boundaries are being violated, and when your human needs, especially in childhood, are not being met. Anger in childhood often emerges when a child is in distress; it's a call for *reconnection*, to draw another back to you, so you feel safe in the warm embrace of a loving relationship. Love is in your nature, as is giving love, but this can easily be shut down if your essential needs are not met, as it no longer seems safe to be in your body or express your emotions.

THE ALCHEMICAL TRANSFORMATION OF ANGER

Your relationship to anger is transformed when you begin to see and feel your anger rather than act it out or stifle it. Taking ownership of your anger transforms it into supportive, life-affirming energy.

This energy can help in your spiritual transformation. Once you can feel its flow and it transforms back into your vital life force, you're connecting deeply to your innermost being. Transmuted anger can become part of the animating force of your fully embodied self.

Take a moment to reflect on your present relationship with anger and your relationship to an embodied spirituality.

- My relationship to anger is:

  _____

  _____

- My relationship to an embodied spirituality is:

  _____

  _____

- As you've worked through your trauma, has your relationship to anger changed in any way?

  _____

  _____

- Has your relationship to your spirituality changed in any way?

_____

_____

THE SCIENCE OF ANGER

Children have a natural impulse for healthy aggression when they are in distress. A child's intense crying alerts caregivers to tend to its needs. This natural emotional system influences social intimacy, but it also incites the deep psychic pain of separation distress that motivates both the caregiver and child to locate each other.[63] If the child in distress is left unattended, it faces conditions that begin to feel life-threatening as the distress increases. Because infants and young children have no capacity or choice for fleeing to safety or fighting, when the child's organism perceives threat, many body systems shut down in a dissociative response.[64] But prior to dissociation, anger is a primary emotional response to the lack of connection and protection.

The anger circuits of a child's brain light up not to strike out at another but as a call for help—to bring a caregiver to their aid.[65] When the caregiver doesn't respond or responds by punishing the child, isolating it, or responding angrily, the child's anger gets repressed or dissociated. As the child grows into adulthood and anger remains unresolved, it becomes transformed into all manner of distorted and negative feelings—such as hatred, self-loathing, blame, and irritability. Unfortunately, these expressions of anger do not satisfy the original need for connection.

False beliefs about anger become crystallized in childhood, and together with associated psychological patterns they may create a false sense of self in relationship to anger.

Anger may have felt frightening to you as a child; your caregivers may have responded with anger . A raging parent may have given you an erroneous notion that equates anger with power. So you refrain from touching your own anger, your own internal power. However, as an adult, you now can face what you couldn't as a child and give yourself what you need.

THE SPLIT-OFF ASPECTS OF ANGER

When anger doesn't feel safe, we split it off or repress it, in either developmental or shock trauma. Feeling anger can be so terrifying that we project it outward or force it inward. When you integrate that split-off anger energy, you can express a healthy level of anger when needed. By safely reclaiming and integrating anger, you regain an internal sense of power.

It's not wise to evoke anger in a workbook. Instead, we will focus on changing your relationship with this emotion. Along with more body awareness, presence, and a greater capacity to feel, you can naturally and gently transform your anger. Sometimes simply touching into an emotion, feeling it within your body, gently, without reactivity, can shift your body to a more self-organizing state.

WHEN LIFE GIVES YOU TOO MUCH TO BEAR

Many individuals with developmental trauma who seek help for trauma-related symptoms find treatment focused on shock or acute traumas. They often don't get the vital help their body and brain needs for recovery.

We took a close look at developmental trauma and its lasting effects in chapters 1 and 3. This emotional neglect and emotional abuse is described as "persistent or extreme thwarting of the child's basic emotional needs, . . . [involving] parental acts that are harmful because they are insensitive to the child's developmental level."[66]

Research has shown that emotional abuse and emotional neglect account for 36 percent and 52 percent of identified child maltreatment cases, respectively.[67] The American Academy of Pediatrics recently acknowledged psychological maltreatment as "the most challenging and prevalent form of child abuse and neglect."[68] Maltreatment of infants and children may produce developmental consequences more severe than other forms of abuse.[69] However, it's also coming to light that children whose needs are not met are suffering an insidious type of neglect that causes a number of symptoms. Rather than focusing on symptoms, you're focusing on solutions, which will help to diminish and dissolve the problem.

THE VALUE OF CURIOSITY

In healing trauma, it's essential to develop mindful awareness of fixed beliefs about yourself and the world. Hold these lightly; be curious. Curiosity softens rigid beliefs and self-judgment. Curiosity is a state of both mind and brain; it develops your capacity for healthy exploration and discovery even when there are difficulties from traumas, enhancing meaning and purpose.[70] When you're curious, you also learn more.[71] You've been developing the capacity of curiosity throughout this workbook.

Curiosity arises when:

- You have increased focus and attention

- You're engaged in a sense of exploration

- Negative emotions and fear subside

- You shift from feeling isolated to being able to engage with others[72]

RELEASING COPING STRATEGIES

People use many coping strategies to numb unpleasant or frightening experiences—smoking, drinking alcohol, unhealthy sexual patterns, overexercising, taking medication, overeating, overworking, any form of addiction—including overdependence on your mobile device. You may realize you have avoidant behaviors, or you may want to stop and look more closely at your actions and behaviors to see if you can recognize them now and over time. Notice any behavior that you use to avoid feeling, emotions, or connecting with yourself or others in any way. Begin a list of avoidant behaviors that you are aware of now; add to it as you become aware of more. Next, be curious about what you are avoiding, and use an exercise in place of the avoidant behavior so you become more present with what you are trying to avoid.

Make a list of any avoidant behaviors you are aware of.

_____

_____

_____

_____

PLACING ANGER AT A SAFE DISTANCE

It can feel like anger is simply too much for you to experience in your body. High arousal energy often binds in the nervous system and organs of infants and children who have no other means to discharge or process it. If you experienced trauma when you were young, this may be so for you. When anger arises and you want to face it and feel it, but it seems too much for your system, a wonderful way to remain with it is to place it at a safe distance until you're better able to tolerate it. To avoid being overwhelmed when anger emerges, try the exercise that follows.

Recently a patient of mine experienced a profound bodily shift as she visualized her anger expressing itself freely over the ocean. As she did so, she felt her organs releasing and relaxing, leaving her feeling empowered and fully accepting anger as her birthright, not needing to lash outward or inward, simply feeling its power as part of her. This energy, with its sense of annihilation, had frightened her for many years. Putting it out there at a safe distance removed the intense fear that had prevented her from facing it fully.

Remember, imagination creates new, unfamiliar possibilities, and as you imagine and feel your body, you're creating new connections in your brain's neuronal pathways. You're giving your anger a place to fully express, safely—without anyone, including yourself, feeling hurt.

If you have an emergence of anger or rage that feels too intense to remain present with, imagine sending it out over the ocean, far enough away that you feel safe. The anger's intensity should lessen. As you see it *out there*, allow it to express itself. Can you sense how it does? Does it take any form—a volcano exploding, or a Tasmanian devil in a raging fury, or an explosion of some sort? Allow it to express fully. Feel your body as you see this happen *out there* on the ocean. The following exercise will lead you through this process.

EXERCISE: Experiencing Anger at a Safe Distance

1. As you feel anger emerging in your body, if it feels overwhelming, imagine seeing it somewhere at a safe distance, such as over the ocean.

2. When the anger is far enough away, allow it to express itself any way it wishes. Observe and feel in your body as you observe it *out there*. Draw from your inner knowing what the anger *out there* most needs to be free and fully expressed.

3. As you imagine the anger expressing itself, stay connected to your body and feel its response. This should lessen the intensity of emotion in your body, allowing you to safely tolerate some of the arousal energy of anger.

4. Once the anger has expressed itself and you feel complete or sense you've had enough, let the image dissolve and feel any sensations of energy moving in your body.

5. Spend a few moments allowing your body to settle by orienting to your surroundings.

6. How was this exercise for you? Were you able to stay connected to the imagery and your body? Describe how it was to feel the energy of anger in your body this way.

_____

_____

_____

_____

Imagine a life in which trauma no longer burdens you. This can happen with the work you're doing. Then you can anticipate triumph and joy. Visualize with an intention for this to be your life. It has been suggested that intention has a direct impact on energy flow.[73]

DEVELOPING YOUR AGENCY

Throughout this workbook you've been developing your self-agency—becoming an effective agent in the world, including your interpersonal world. You foster this as you enhance self-esteem and self-efficacy and develop self-mastery in different areas of your life; for instance:

- You're becoming master of your emotions, meaning they no longer control you, but you experience them while staying present with them.

- You're gaining mastery over your feelings toward yourself, recognizing any signs of self-loathing or criticism; you can see that they arise from the failed environment of your past, and you can access compassion as an antidote or transform the underlying feelings of unresolved anger.

If patterns of self-negation are continuing;

- Notice them.

- Keep them at a distance; don't give them any fuel by engaging.

- Turn your attention to another task.

Eventually the self-negating will settle down, no longer bothering you. Concurrently, you're developing your unique and strong sense of self.

YOUR CONTRIBUTION TO YOUR WORLD

The world isn't happening to you, even if it sometimes feels that way. You're contributing your inner environment to the world, and you can make the world a more loving place. Imagination is a great tool to develop this knowing and sense of self, as you'll see in the following exercises.

EXERCISE: Your Proactive Sense of Agency

Part 1

You're going to recall a time, situation, conflict, or person that evokes the experience of anger. This time you'll imagine you are proactive, not reactive, responding with internal power and a quiet strength, transmuting the anger in your body. You're the alchemist who transforms the destructive element of anger into its golden form—internal power and strength—in your body vessel.

1. As you recall the anger-evoking scene in your mind, experience the anger as a deep heat or force that flows through your body. Maybe you imagine a color, like red, and as it moves through you don't allow any of this energy/anger to lash out. You firmly stand your ground, breathing into your belly, feeling the energy flowing until your body straightens and you feel a deep internal power. As you imagine, stay connected to body awareness.

2. From this place of internal power, feeling it or imagining you feel it, imagine how you'd like to calmly or assertively respond. Visualize this as clearly as you can, using all your senses to bring it to life.

3. Take triumph in your newly created situation. As you see yourself responding, feel your body and feel or imagine feeling your internal power, strength, and confidence.

4. See yourself responding in a way that makes you feel good about yourself or proud.

5. Notice how and where you feel that goodness and pride in your body.

6. Remain with these good feelings for at least 45 seconds if you can. Feeling informs thought.

Part 2

If your effort in part 1 didn't leave you feeling good about yourself, try again with different anger-evoking scenes. Once you feel you've realized the benefit of part 1, proceed with this next part:

1. Feel how much you like yourself in this newly empowering way of responding. As you feel good about yourself, notice your body.

2. Can you feel proud of yourself with the scene you just created? If not, find another time in which you felt proud of yourself for doing something effectively.

3. Once you complete this with one scene, generate another and repeat the process. This will reinforce positive feelings about yourself.

4. Describe your experience.

_____

_____

_____

The more you focus on the positive feelings, the clearer and more accessible they will become. Soon you'll naturally feel strong and positive feelings about yourself. With practice, you'll be able to access positive feelings without the imagery.

Part 3

Once positive feelings are familiar to you and rooted in your body and body awareness:

1. Choose a situation in which you usually *don't* feel good, proud, or positive about yourself.

2. Imagine yourself in it now and evoke positive feelings—the opposite of self-doubt (confidence), self-negation (assertion or self-worth), self-loathing (self-love or appreciation).

3. Evoke compassion and loving kindness to fully accept all that you are.

4. See your scene playing out; feel positive and good about yourself. Root those feelings in your body and see yourself responding in ways in which you really feel good about yourself.

Part 4

1. Imagine a time and scene in the near future in which you always have access to feeling good about yourself, know self-compassion, and can respond proactively rather than react.

2. Imagine you've always felt this way. This feeling has always been here and has now surfaced into your awareness, so you always have clear access to this authentic expression of your innermost self.

3. See yourself as clearly as you can; feel your body as you do so.

4. Delight in simply being who you truly are.

5. Smile, even slightly, as you imagine and feel. Stay with the experience for a minute or longer if you're able.

6. Describe your experience.

_____

_____

_____

_____

WHAT I LEARNED IN THIS CHAPTER

Write out any thoughts or experiences you have about using anger to transform your consciousness.

_____

_____

_____

_____

_____

_____

CHAPTER 11

Witness and Receive the Universe

Your heart's desire is like the notion of the Sanskrit term *dharma*. Dharma points to the cosmic order that makes life possible. It's energetically connected to the current of your individual life force. There is a vector in dharma that naturally moves you into harmony with a rhythm that ties you to something greater. As you come into relationship with this, both outwardly and inwardly, you'll feel more fulfilled. Even when things are challenging, you'll experience life unfolding with leisure and ease as you continue your healing journey.

The concept of dharma includes conduct/behaviors and virtues that constitute a "right way of living"—actions in accord with presence and a *universal flow of life*. Accordingly, everything and everyone has its place in the cosmos. When you experience this personally, the momentum and flow of dharma instills a quiet inner joy.

This chapter continues to explore what gets in the way of your expressing your authentic self so that you can do so. We'll explore body movement using the ancient wisdom philosophy of Sri Vidya. If it's new to you, rest assured you need know only what I present here. I learned this wonderful movement form from a teacher in this tradition. It may bring you a fresh approach, opening new possibilities for healing.

PAUSE FOR REFLECTION: Your Authentic Self

Knowing and being connected to your heart's deepest longing kindles an unseen, subtly felt energy that helps you move away from your traumatized self—the self that keeps you locked into old patterns, beliefs, and behaviors—toward greater fulfillment and self-expression. This is a reciprocal relationship; the more you recognize and connect to your dharma, the more likely you are to be drawn to that which is healing, that which leads to your authentic expression.

YOUR SUBTLE BODY

There's another reciprocal relationship: the subtle body can regulate or dysregulate the physical body, and vice versa. Reflect on the following questions:

- Are you aware of your heart's deepest desire, or what it is to be in your dharma?

- Do you remember a time when you felt in the flow of life, with a sense of presence?

- Are you beginning to experience this more now that you're addressing trauma through body awareness and have developed your capacity for self-observation and inquiry? If yes, describe this. It can be as simple as feeling present, confident, more solidity in your body; an impulse to be a writer, parent, or scholar; or feeling deeply connected to your own essence and authenticity.

_____

_____

_____

- At this point in the workbook, do you have a different sense of
  your authentic self than when you began?   **Yes   No**

- How does this feel? Focus on all the positive changes that you notice, using as much descriptive language as possible.

_____

_____

_____

- When you're not in your authentic self, when you feel insincere or misaligned with your true inner self, what can you do to begin shifting back to authenticity? How is it for you?

_____

_____

_____

- Are you aware of any way in which you still feel you influence or manipulate the environment to feel safe or comfortable? For example:

  - Project authority onto others.

  - Act aloof to hide your vulnerability.

  - Attempt to control others.

  - Overly compliment others so they like you.

  - Act out all the conclusions you've made about the world; for instance:

    - Reject others first for fear of being rejected.

    - Betray others to prevent being betrayed.

  - Please others so they will like you or you don't upset them.

  - Avoid expressing yourself in a way that could cause conflict.

  _____

  _____

  _____

- If you use any of these or other ways of being not truly authentic, what do you imagine happening if you didn't manipulate the environment, if you were truly authentic and operating from your inner truth?

  _____

  _____

  _____

- If you could be *doing* or *being* anything, what would that be right now? Make this at least 50-percent achievable and believable in relationship to who you are and your current circumstances.

  _____

  _____

  _____

- Clearly see yourself enjoying the fruit of your heart's desire—being your most authentic self. The root of your heart's desire is to know you are love. If that's not clear to you yet, first imagine what loving yourself would feel like. Your heart's desire will naturally flow from that. It is not an action but a way of being.

_____

_____

_____

_____

When you're living with the ongoing effects of trauma, your most authentic voice remains in its shadows, waiting in silence. Living from your authentic self reduces anxiety, fear, shame, and guilt. When you live more authentically, your thoughts, beliefs, emotions, words, and actions emerge from deep within you. You can stay true to a naturally confident, genuine, vital way of being without much effort—you're in your dharma. You're secure enough emotionally and physically that you've no desire or need to manipulate the world around you to feel safe. Comfortable in yourself, you're released from any internal or external pressure to act or appear in any prescribed way. What a relief to not have to be *somebody!*

As you nurture the inner conditions necessary for deep-rooted recovery, your inherent capacity for healing will unfold and your heart's desire will become clear. Even if you don't know how that expresses right now, it will come within reach.

SETTING AN INTENTION: SANKALPA

Setting an intention can bring clarity and focus to your healing process. You did this at the beginning of the workbook. Now revisit that intention to see how it unfolded over time. Are you ready for a new intention(s) yet? If being connected to your heart's desire feels important right now, you can set an intention to make this part of your continuing healing process.

Your awareness and focus allow you to recognize the rich texture of your life; they spur choice and change. With a strong sense of presence, you can choose, and set in motion, a different pattern or way of being. The power of your consciousness can shift the energy flow of your moods and emotions. Intention also directly affects this.[74] Your life force becomes stronger and more powerful as you clear the erroneous beliefs and survival strategies that have been quietly sabotaging your ability to create your best life. If there are still areas in which you feel stuck, the consciousness of your presence combined with intention can free you from them. Record some intentions here or in your journal.

- My intention through the healing process is to: _____

  _____

- My intention is to: _____

  _____

Now, change your intentions to a *sankalpa*—in the yogic tradition, a formula for realizing your heart's desire. The term comes from the Sanskrit roots *san* ("connection with the highest truth"), and *kalpa* ("a vow"). It's a resolve to focus on a specific goal that can be psychological or philosophical. As you focus your intention, a sankalpa harnesses your will to harmonize your mind and body.

A sankalpa is stated as a positive affirmation in the present; for instance: "I'm living in harmony with my heart's deepest desire." It's better to be specific and name exactly what you would like. For instance: "I'm joyously in contact with my body, emotions, and other loving people."

- I am _____

Once you have clear intentions and a powerful sankalpa, repeat them before and after your meditations. When you're in a meditative state, you're in a deeper connection to the universal life force. Here you connect to a depth of consciousness beyond your rational mind that enhances your intentions.

THE SUBTLE DANCE OF THE UNIVERSE WITHIN YOU

Now we will explore movement—movement that arises from within and moves you. This kind of expressive body movement can help bring what lies beneath your conscious awareness to the surface. Acting as a gateway to the dimension of yourself where words are often inadequate, this spontaneous movement tells a story through the language of dance. This type of whole-body expression can be dramatically satisfying and meaningful.

Dance can mark and deepen the changes you're experiencing in healing your trauma as it facilitates more embodied integration. The meeting of conscious and unconscious in this spontaneous, unchoreographed dance (which I will explain shortly) can move you from disconnection or fragmentation to wholeness and safety in your body. As you begin to move, your thinking eases. As the dance expresses what is difficult to express in words, any internal chatter is drawn into the softness of the dance, and you understand what is being uttered from within through the movement. Dancing in this way can take you into a deeper meditative state. As you feel the movement of your dance, something new emerges, yielding a spiritual rebirth.

THE DANCE OF THE COSMOS

The name of the dance I'll be describing—Lasya Tandava—comes from the Hindu tradition of Sri Vidya. Dancing in Indian culture is regarded as experiencing union with the source of creation—from which, according to many spiritual traditions, we are not separate.

Tandava is thought of as a celestial dance performed by Lord Shiva, who represents the masculine aspect of pure consciousness. Traditionally, Tandava is known as Lord Shiva's dance of destruction. Shakti—the feminine aspect of pure consciousness or creation—performs her dance, Lasya, in response. Her soft, harmonizing movement brings an end to destruction and moves toward assimilation. You can see the connection between these dances and healing trauma—the shift from what was destructive to what is harmonizing. Lasya Tandava imparts an inner grace and beauty that is delightful to feel. This is what you'll be aiming for.

THE GIFT OF LASYA

Lasya Tandava isn't about being somebody. Most of your everyday movements are born of interactions that support your being somebody—from the way you walk, to housework, to self-care. Lasya Tandava breaks this habit. As all your identities—who you thought you should be or need to be—drop away, even momentarily, you may experience a sense of relief in *not being* someone—enabling you to more fully express your authentic self.

This practice allows energetic movements that acute or shock trauma may have stopped or distorted to be completed and integrated, slowly and gently. As body tensions soften through the dance, your life force brings a renewed fluidity to your subtle and physical body. When you're in the movement, it may seem quite natural to feel the subtle energy, but later you may wonder *who was moving?*—a good question to simply contemplate.

Lasya Tandava embodies the tenderness and grace of the cosmos within you. When your emotions feel too volatile or the energies of your meditative or breathing practices too full, use Lasya Tandava to express these emotions softly and gently. It is also a wonderful moving meditation.

INTEGRATING YOUR EMOTIONS

If you practice hatha yoga (which I wholeheartedly recommend), you may know it prepares and helps the body to move energetic blockages. Lasya Tandava goes further than yoga in working with energy by bringing more fluidity and spontaneity into the movements. This supportive practice helps you integrate both the energy that you're softening and dislodging the trauma-created body tensions and the life force you're generating through your healing practices. This includes integrating emotions.

In this process, you're embracing a larger sense of purpose in your life and awareness of yourself as part of a greater whole—a common spiritual teaching for thousands of years. As your perspectives expand, you're cultivating an embodied and interconnected nature. Movement is a wonderful means to deepen this process.

FEELING YOUR ESSENCE

To borrow again from the Indian tradition, when you're listening to music and your energy begins to move you, sense or look for a certain *rasa* ("essence" or "taste"), which points to an aesthetic flavor that dance or music invokes; an emotional tone difficult to express in words for the one listening or watching (or performing). I describe it as resonating in the octave of one's deepest truth. Rasas are created by your state of mind, which transports you to the essence of your consciousness and can reflect your spirituality. This raises the questions: Who was dancing? Who was moving?

Before you begin this next exercise, find a piece of slow, melodic music without much of a beat. It should touch your heart, drawing out a rasa that you can feel throughout your body as you listen. Try different pieces of music to find one that feels right for you. I suggest you explore music from India, as we are drawing from one of its traditions.

Find a space in which you can have some undisturbed private time, with room to move around unconstrained. You can stand or sit, whatever feels right as you follow your body. Let the movement come spontaneously and naturally from within rather than moving from the intention of your thoughts or habitual actions.

In this dance, you're breaking your habitual patterns of movement. Eventually, your body becomes free from the memories of engraved patterns and incomplete movements that don't serve you, and you find an authentic expression. As a result, your everyday expression becomes more authentic. Ultimately, you'll realize there is no separation between the dance and the dancer; you, your body's energies, and the cosmos are one and the same.

You may feel a pulsing sensation at your sacrum; you may feel like your breath is being breathed here; you may hear a sound within the breath. This is wonderful! You're connecting to the rarefied field of subtle life force—the principle underlying every living thing that connects you to the energy of the cosmos.

EXERCISE: The Practice of Lasya Tandava

1. Begin either standing, feet hip width apart, or sitting in a meditation posture with legs crossed.

2. Play your piece or pieces of music.

3. Focusing deeply on your lower abdomen or as close to the pubic bone as you can, feel as if the breath is being breathed down there. Try placing your hand on your pubic bone and see if you can get the breath to move there.

4. Make sure your face is soft and your body relaxed, and that the breath is breathing you without effort.

5. Lift and release your perineum (between the anus and genitals) a few times, toning this area and bringing energy and awareness here. Often the movement of energy begins from the lower abdominal area, but not always.

6. Pause and feel how the music resonates with your body's subtle energy.

7. You may notice an impulse to move. Allow it to move you, slowly, possibly in unfamiliar ways. You may initially feel it only in your hands or arms, or in your whole body. Simply follow the movement.

8. If you don't feel the impulse to move, very slowly initiate some movement to see if you can catch the wave of internal energy flow. Remember, this is a practice; not everyone will get it the first time.

9. Once you initiate movement, be sure it emerges without your control, so that rather than moving your body intentionally, your body *is* moved. Don't choose what movement you make; follow the movement as it emerges.

10. Allow your energy to move your physical body as you surrender to something that cannot be explained, exactly repeated, or sought after.

11. Enjoy the softness and gentleness of the practice, and the quieting of mind.

12. You can play the music several times or use a few different pieces of music. When it ends, allow yourself to come into stillness.

13. In the stillness, simply be aware of your body, the quiet of your mind, and any energy flow (it will likely be very subtle).

14. Remain in this state for as long as you're able to.

15. Movement followed by writing about it can expand your experience. Describe it here:

_____

_____

_____

_____

_____

_____

SPIRITUALITY AND CONNECTION

Richard Rohr, in his book *The Divine Dance*, wrote eloquently about the revolution that is diminishing the old structures of religious institutions that no longer work. He observes that many aspects of religion no longer offer, or are missing, what many people are searching for today—an *innate sense of spirituality*. He says that "the greatest dis-ease facing humanity right now is our profound and painful sense of disconnection."[75] How right he is!

Rohr believes that it's not just our disconnection from God that is problematic in modern religion, but our disconnection from ourselves and our bodies, from one another and the world around us. Exactly what you've been discovering. Reconnecting with your body, yourself, others, the world, and beyond, fosters an innate and embodied spirituality, corresponding to the flow of your own life force energy that you embody through practices and integration.

You are likely becoming more courageously willing and able to see your patterns and behavior, to recognize your outgrown identities and survival strategies. Write here about any deepening awareness of these and your experience of facing them and allowing them to dissolve or diminish.

_____

_____

_____

_____

_____

WRITING A LOVING LETTER TO YOURSELF

Handwrite a loving letter to yourself, appreciating all the work you've done on your journey of resolving trauma so far. As you write, stay connected to your feelings. Notice how they deepen, shift, morph, expand, and lead you into knowing more about what you need and who you are. If emotions emerge as you write, pause and give yourself time to acknowledge and feel them.

1. Begin by creating a sacred space—perhaps light a candle or say a prayer of gratitude.

2. As you begin the letter, acknowledge all the places you've shown up for yourself and all the frightening places you've touched into.

3. Acknowledge how you may have opened your heart and allowed more love to emanate as you and through you.

4. Acknowledge the difficulties you've endured from trauma as well as those you may still be working on.

5. Acknowledge the fear you've faced, the anger you've transformed, and the courage you've shown.

6. Be especially caring to yourself; nurture yourself with your words. What words were once missing in your life that could nurture those parts of you that still need those words now? Attune to yourself to know what you would most like to hear that would be most loving and supportive. Find words, phrases, sentences that are:

- Supportive

- Loving

- Nurturing

- Nourishing

- Self-honoring

- Sweet

- Encouraging

7. Listen to yourself. Witness yourself. Deeply connect with yourself.

8. Inspire yourself to continue to do your healing work and to continue with the practices you've learned.

9. Become your own support system; encourage yourself to live the life you want to live, to feel fully alive, spontaneous, and joyous. You can create this life; it's waiting for you. Now write!

_____

_____

_____

_____

_____

_____

_____

_____

10. How was the experience of writing a loving and supportive letter to yourself? Describe how you feel after it's written, and you've read over it at least once. Describe any insights you gained from writing the letter.

_____

_____

_____

WRITING A LOVING LETTER TO YOUR BODY

Since you began this workbook, I imagine you have a renewed relationship to your body to some degree. As you write your letter, stay connected with your body awareness, pausing for any new feeling. Your body may respond as you acknowledge it. Write your letter knowing you're still healing your relationship with your body. You may want to begin with something you're grateful for or an overall deep sense of gratitude; you may begin with an apology for the difficulties it has gone through and acknowledge your process of reconnection.

1. Find a quiet space where you won't be disturbed.

2. Light a candle or do something that represents opening a sacred space for you to write this letter.

3. Feel into your body; feel into the relationship you now have with your body.

4. Write from the depth of your authentic voice.

_____

_____

_____

_____

_____

_____

5. When you feel the letter is complete, pause and spend some time with yourself, your body, your whole experience.

6. Write about your experience.

_____

_____

_____

_____

_____

_____

_____

_____

Well done! Congratulations for all that you've experienced on your journey. How do you feel as you come to the end of the book? Although you may not be going through the book in a linear fashion, you are here now, perhaps at a point of completing all the exercises. Of course, the exercises are meant to be revisited over and over. I find that as people advance in their psychospiritual maturity, they naturally revisit traumatic or wounding events or periods. We heal in layers that go through the depth of our being. Each time you revisit an event, if necessary, you reach a new level of healing.

The book conclusion is about celebrating you and encouraging you to put together a daily practice if you haven't already done so. I deeply acknowledge all the remarkable work you've accomplished and will accomplish. You are truly amazing!

CONCLUSION

Your Daily Practice:
The Key to Resolving Trauma

On our journey together through this workbook, you've explored many aspects of trauma and learned exercises that can help you heal and resolve your trauma. You know that PTG is possible—that you can become *more than* you were prior to any trauma. Through practicing the exercises, you've released, or begun to release, the frozen energy of trauma and connected with your authentic self and spiritual nature. You can direct your mind energy and the life force of your physical and subtle bodies toward the life you really want to live.

The journey of healing trauma is to become a more spontaneous and embodied being—an integrated and interconnected self. You've learned and practiced ways to self-regulate when difficulties arise and now have a rich array of practices you can use to cultivate the positive qualities of compassion, loving kindness, and gratitude. You've discovered your unique inner qualities and authentic expressions. To embody these qualities requires gathering and assimilating split-off parts of your consciousness. Patterns and erroneous beliefs have prevented your being fully aware of and in touch with your physical body. Through using your breath, presence, imagination, awareness and movement you can overcome those obstacles.

It's likely that you're now more resourceful, resilient, confident, and upright. You're on your way to knowing directly that your body holds inherent wisdom; that your essence is love. When you live from these innate qualities, you reach your heart's desire and can live in a flow of presence. Perhaps you can sense the harmony and energy arising from the connectedness you've cultivated.

This may have been and continue to be a painful birth and delivery. The challenge can be also be energizing and exciting. I hope you've gotten in touch with a conscious yearning for what you desire from your opening heart. I hope you're better able to risk facing your fears for the sake of love and an inner sense of freedom and wholeness.

I know this hasn't been an easy journey; your tears may still be falling; you may be hurting, burning, screaming. Anger may still grab you; rage may terrify you. Sadness and grief can feel insurmountable. It may feel like your suffering will last forever. I assure you, it doesn't have to!

I encourage you to find other trusted people who can support you. There are more resources available, as the inner world of trauma and insights for healing are being discovered, recognized, and acknowledged by many people. I hope you're inspired to stay on this healing path, to continue to take the next step and discover the fruits of your perseverance and commitment to your practices.

You know now that it takes courage, determination, and creativity to transform the experiences of trauma into something meaningful and beautiful. It takes a passion for life to stay on the uncharted course of your healing. I have deep respect for you and your courage in this journey. I know how terrible trauma can be—and how exhilarated and empowered you'll feel when you've healed from its devastating effects. My own inner life, enriched from healing trauma and having a sustained spiritual practice, has become expansive, vibrant, and quietly joyful. I've found the innate essence of love that lies within us all, the infinite vastness of the cosmos, and the multiple dimensions in between. We are the cosmos *and* the embodied self.

Now imagine that you're opening to many new chapters of your life—chapters full of self-reverence and respect for your sacred journey. Acknowledge yourself for all that you've done. Be gentle and generous toward yourself. Keep practicing the exercises that work for you. Keep touching back into the basics, always. They provide the solid ground that keeps you connected to your body and helps you continue to build resilience and resolution. Honor the sanctity of your life. Return daily to practicing gratitude and loving kindness. It's up to you to use the skills and ideas you've learned to continue cultivating a life of compassion, presence, and awareness.

In this, compassion will be your greatest ally. When you awaken to compassion and take it as your perspective, you may recognize that all suffering *is* compassion, obscured from its source by early wounding and trauma. As the light of compassion shines on the suffering elements of your consciousness, ultimately you will find integration and wholeness and a profound personal understanding, with new meaning and a new life story.

Life is full of experiences, heartwarming and heartbreaking. You can meet them all in a state of presence and openness. Healing trauma and awakening to your most essential nature isn't only about feeling good; it's about meeting, being with, and allowing all your human expressions and experiences to flow through you. Nothing needs to stick; everything changes. However, even amid ongoing change, there is a level of mind that is unchanging, unbounded, in which all of life is displayed. You may have already touched into this. If you haven't, you can open up to this by continuing with your practices.

Observe your inner life. Continue to notice patterns and strategies that no longer serve you. Thank them, and they will be released as you do your work. Reject no parts of yourself. Have compassion for yourself—for the you who was let down by life circumstances, or experienced devastation or shock through traumatic events, or was hurt and abandoned by others. Through instinct you adapted ways to survive. Transformation happens as you accept all of who you are.

Many of us labor under a misconception of ourselves and the world as divided; we fail to see and experience our natural wholeness. This creates a sense of separation from the world. As you learn to perceive through a larger lens and embrace your body as an integral part of your human experience, this misperception, this confusion, dissolves. Who's to say that this is not exactly how it's meant to be—that trauma is not a pathway that helps you awaken to fully knowing who you are? There is unquestionably a gift in healing trauma that allows you to embrace all of being human.

DESIGNING YOUR PRACTICE

Because healing trauma and embodiment are an ongoing process and a way of life, I encourage you to design a daily practice. The following is an example from which you can draw a possible schedule.

- Upon waking, hand on your heart, practice loving kindness. Express this spiritual gesture for embodied love.

- If you feel sluggish, practice one or two of the pranayamas.

- Before you get busy, spend a few minutes expressing, out loud or silently, five things you're grateful for. Pause to feel the effects in your body/mind.

- At lunch, find a few minutes to do your proprioceptive exercise—feeling your body in time and space.

- At any time, you can place your hand on your heart and check in with how you feel—connect with your body and feel what is *here now*. Practice radically accepting what is.

- Strengthen your boundaries during the day. Practice saying no!

- When you feel anxious, ungrounded, numb, or disconnected, do your orienting and grounding exercises. Say "Aum" out loud three times, with a long exhale. Practice alternate nostril breathing. Reach out to others for support. Express what you need.

- Connect every day in some way with yourself, your body, others, and nature. Reach out to someone to connect to.

- At the end of the day, practice pranayama.

- Before sleep, practice compassion and gratitude.

- Listen to an online recording in the evening or have it memorized, so you can practice without listening.

- Write loving letters to yourself.

- Dance slowly and allow your subtle body to soften your tensions and integrate your life energy.

- Return to your list of resources, including the ones you'd like to create, and imagine what you can do to bring those resources to life through your intention and heartfelt action. Cultivate them.

I wish you ease and grace on your healing journey.

Acknowledgments

I acknowledge my deep gratitude for the many body-oriented psychotherapies and traditions of spiritual development that have deeply influenced my life and work.

I offer special thanks to my family: Sam; and my wonderful daughter, Sapphire. And many thanks to my dear friends who offered their love and support: Ronald Hoffman, Simmi Goyle, Cherie Rolap, and Andrei Novac. Their encouragement was unwavering. I am grateful to Sandra Easter, who helped with the editing, and Laura Weissman, who also supported me in the initial stages of the book. And great thanks to Zaya and Maurizio Benazzo, founders of Science and Nonduality, who offered me a place to share my passion for spirituality and trauma. Special thanks to Lisa Genova, for her kindness in writing the foreword for this book.

I'd like to thank my clients and patients, from whom I was privileged to learn so much about the darkness and despair of trauma and the passage back into light and love.

There are many teachers that I am very grateful for, including Bessel van der Kolk, Peter Levine, Laurence Heller, Daniel P. Brown, Diana Fosha, Dianne Poole Heller, and Parvathi Nanda Nath, who have contributed to my understanding of trauma and of the knowing of the true nature of mind.

Thank you to New Harbinger Publications, especially Elizabeth Hollis Hansen, Jennifer Holder, and Kristi Hein, for their support in making this book a reality.

Notes

1. Tedeschi, R., J. Shakespeare-Finch, K. Taku, and L. G. Calhoun. 2018. *Post Traumatic Growth: Theory, Research and Application.* New York: Routledge.

2. Schore, A. N. 2012. *The Science of the Art of Psychotherapy.* New York: Norton.

3. Stapp, H. 2017. *Quantum Theory and Free Will: How Mental Interventions Translate into Bodily Action.* Berkeley, CA: Springer Intl.

4. Ibid.

5. Steele, K., S. Boon, and O. Hart. 2017. *Treating Trauma-Related Dissociation: A Practical, Integrative Approach.* New York: Norton.

6. Porges, S. W. 2011. *The Polyvagal Theory: Neurophysiological Foundation of Emotions, Attachment, Communication and Self-Regulation.* New York: Norton.

7. Ibid.

8. McGilchrist, I. 2009. *The Master and His Emissary: The Divided Brain and the Making of the Western World.* New Haven, CT: Yale University Press.

9. Siegel, D. J. 2010. *Mindsight: The New Science of Personal Transformation.* New York: Bantam Books.

10. Yehuda, R., and et al. 2014. "Influences of Maternal and Paternal PYSD on Epigenetic Regulation of the Glucocortoid Receptor Gene in Holocaust Survivor Offspring." *American Journal of Psychiatry* 171: 827–880.

11. Ibid.

12. Badenock, B. 2018. *The Heart of Trauma: Healing the Embodied Brain in the Context of Relationships.* New York: Norton.

13. Porges, S. W. 2011. *The Polyvagal Theory: Neurophysiological Foundation of Emotions, Attachment, Communication and Self-Regulation.* New York: Norton.

14. Steele, K., S. Boon, and O. Hart. 2017. *Treating Trauma-Related Dissociation: A Practical, Integrative Approach*. New York: Norton.

15. Ibid.

16. Siegel, D. J. 2010. *Mindsight: The New Science of Personal Transformation*. New York: Bantam Books.

17. Scaer, R. C. 2005. *The Trauma Spectrum: Hidden Wounds and Human Resilience*. New York: Norton.

18. Porges, *The Polyvagal Theory*.

19. Paris, G. 2007. *Wisdom of the Psyche: Depth Psychology after Neuroscience*, p. 205. New York: Routledge.

20. Porges, *The Polyvagal Theory*.

21. van der Kolk, B. A. 2014. *The Body Keeps the Score: Mind, Brain and Body in the Transformation of Trauma*. Berkeley, CA: Penguin.

22. Putnam, F. W. 1992. "Discussion: Are Alter Personalities Fragments or Figments?" *Psychoanalytic Inquiry* (http://dx.doi.org/10.1080/07351699209533884) 12 (1): 95–111, p. 104.

23. Porges, *The Polyvagal Theory*.

24. Scaer, *The Trauma Spectrum*.

25. McGilchrist, I. 2009. *The Master and His Emissary: The Divided Brain and the Making of the Western World*. New Haven, CT: Yale University Press, p. 235.

26. Wilkinson, M. 2006. *Coming into Mind: The Mind-Brain Relationship; A Jungian Clinical Perspective*. New York: Routledge.

27. Jung, C. G. 1928/1966. *The Collected Works of C. G. Jung*, 2nd ed. Edited by H. Read, M. Fordham, G. Adler and W. McGuire. Vol. 16. Princeton University Press, pp. 131–132.

28. Scannapieco, M., and K. Connell-Carrik. 2005. *Understanding Child Maltreatment: An Ecological and Developmental Perspective*. New York: Oxford University Press.

29. Schore, *The Science of the Art of Psychotherapy*.

30. Gerbarg, P. L., P. R. Muskin, and R. P. Brown. 2017. *Complementary and Integrative Treatments in Psychiatric Practice*. Arlington, VA: American Psychiatric Publishing.

31. Shaffer, F., R. McCraty, and C. L. Zerr. 2014. "A Healthy Heart Is Not a Metronome: An Integrative Review of the Heart's Anatomy and Heart Rate Variabilty." *Frontiers in Psychology* (doi: org/10.3389/fpsy.2014.01040) 5 (1040).

32. Badenock, *The Heart of Trauma.*

33. Brown, R. P., P. L. Gerbarg, and F. Muench. 2013. "Breathing Practices for Treatment of Psychiatric Stress-Related Medical Conditions." *The Psychiatric Clinics of North America* (doi: 10.1016/j.psc.2013.01.001) 36 (1): 121–140.

34. Gerbarg, Muskin, and Brown, *Complementary and Integrative Treatments.*

35. Porges, *The Polyvagal Theory.*

36. Brown, R. P., and P. L. Gerbarg. 2005. "Sudarshan Kriya Yogic Breathing in Treatment of Stress, Anxiety, and Depression. Part 1 - Neurophysiologic Model." *The Journal of Alternative and Complimentary Medicine* (http://dx.doi.org/10.1089/acm.2005.11.189) 11 (1): 189–201.

37. Porges, S. W., and C. S. Carter. 2017. "Polyvagal Theory and the Social Engagement System." In *Complementary and Integrative Treatments in Psychiatric Practice*, by P. L. Gerbarg, P. R. Muskin, and R. P. Brown. Arlington, VA: American Psychiatric Publishing.

38. Büssing, A., A. G. Wirth, F. Reiser, A. Zahn, K. Humbroich, K. Gerbershagen, and K. Baumann. 2014. "Experience of Gratitude, Awe and Beauty in Life among Patients with Multiple Sclerosis and Psychiatric Disorders." *Health and Quality of Life Outcomes* (http://dx.doi.org/10.1186/14777525-12-63) 12 (63).

39. Mills, P. J., L. Redwine, K. Wilson, M. A. Pung, K. Chinh, B. H. Greenberg, O. Lunde, A. Maisel, and A. Raisinghani. 2015. "Spirituality in Clinical Practice." *American Psychological Association* (http://dx.doi.org/10.1037/scp0000050) 2 (1).

40. Hasenkamp, W., and J. R. White. 2012. *The Monastery and the Microscope: Conversation with the Dalai Lama on Mind, Mindfulness, and the Nature of Reality.* New Haven, CT: Yale University Press.

41. Goleman, D., and R. J. Davidson. 2017. *Altered Traits: Science Reveals How Meditation Changes Your Mind, Brain, and Body.* New York: Avery.

42. Goleman and Davidson, *Altered Traits.*

43. Siegel, D. J. 2007. *The Mindful Brain: Reflection and Attunement in the Cultivation of Well-Being.* New York: Norton, p. 321.

44. Goleman and Davidson, *Altered Traits*.

45. Hasenkamp and White, *The Monastery and the Microscope*.

46. Ibid.

47. Brown, D. P., and D. S. Elliott. 2016. *Attachment Disturbances in Adults: Treatment for Comprehensive Repair*. New York: Norton.

48. Ibid.

49. Gethin, A., and B. Macgregor. 2017. *Helping Baby Sleep: The Science and Practice of Gentle Bedtime Parenting*. Berkley, CA: Ten Speed Press.

50. Bugental, D. B., G. A. Martorell, and V. Barraza. 2003. "The Hormonal Costs of Subtle Forms of Infant Maltreatment." *Hormones and Behavior* (http://dx .doi.org/10.1016/S0018 -506X(02)00008-9) 43 (1): 237–244.

51. Meinischmidt, G., and C. Heim. 2007. "Sensitivity to Intranasal Oxytocin in Adult Men with Early Prenatal Separations." *Biological Psychiatry* 61 (1): 1109–1111.

52. Panksepp, J. 2006. "On the Neuro-Evolutionary Nature of Social Pain, Support, and Empathy." In *Pain: New Essays on Its Nature and the Methodology of Its Study*, by M. Ayded (Ed.). Cambridge, MA: MIT Press.

53. Narvaez, D., J. Panksepp, A. Schore, and T. R. Gleason. 2013. "The Value of Using an Evolutionary Framework for Gauging Children's Well-Being." In *Evolution, Early Experience and Human Development: From Research to Practice and Policy*, by D. Navaez, J. Panksepp, A. Schore, and T. R. Gleason (Eds.). New York: Oxford University Press.

54. Schore, *The Science of the Art of Psychotherapy*; Porges, The Polyvagal Theory.

55. Heller, L., and A. LaPierre. 2012. *Healing Developmental Trauma: How Early Trauma Affects Self-Regulation, Self-Image, and the Capacity for Relationship*. Berkeley, CA: North Atlantic.

56. Brown, Gerbarg, and Muench, "Breathing Practices."

57. Bluhm, R. L., P. C. Williamson, E. A. Osuch, P. A. Frewen, T. K. Stevens, K. Boksman, and R. A. Lanius. 2009. "Alteration in Default Network Connectivity in Posttraumatic Stress Disorder Related to Early-Life Trauma." *Journal of Psychiatry and Neuroscience* 34 (3): 187–194.

58. Steele, Boon, and Hart, *Treating Trauma-Related Dissociation*.

59. Brown and Elliott, *Attachment Disturbances in Adults*.

60. Ibid.

61. Ibid.

62. Wilber, K. 2006. *Integral Spirituality*. Boston, MA: Shambala.

63. Panksepp, *On the Neuro-Evolutionary Nature of Social Pain*.

64. Schore, *The Science of the Art of Psychotherapy*.

65. Panksepp and Biven, *The Archaeology of Mind*.

66. Barnett, D., J. T. Manly, and D. Cicchetti. 1993. *Defining Child Maltreatment: The Interface Between Policy and Research*. Vol. 8, in *Child Abuse, Child Development, and Social Policy: Advances in Developmental Psychology*, by D. Cicchetti and S. L. Toth (Eds.). Norwood, NJ: Ablex, p. 67.

67. Chamberland, C., B. Fallon, T. Black, and N. Trocme. 2011. "Emotional Maltreatment in Canada: Prevalence, Reporting and Child Welfare Responses (CIS2)." *Child Abuse & Neglect* (http://dx.doi.org/10.1016/j.chiabu.2011.03.010) 35: 841–854.

68. Spinazzola, J., H. Hodgdon, J. D. Ford, E. C. Briggs, L. Liang, C. M. Layne, and B. Stolbach. 2014. "Unseen Wounds: The Contribution of Psychological Maltreatment to Child and Adolescent Mental Health Risk Outcomes." *Psychological Trauma: Theory, Research, Practice, and Policy* (http://dx.doi.org10.1037/a0037766) 6 (51): 518–528.

69. Spinazzola et al., "Unseen Wounds."

70. Hill, R., and E. Rossi. 2018. "The Practitioner's Guide to Mirroring Hands: A Client-Responsive Therapy That Facilitates Natural Problem-Solving and Mind-Body Healing." *The Nuntius Nuclei. A Neuroscience for Curiosity* (https://www.thescienceofpsychotherapy.com/nuntius-nuclei-new-neuroscience-curiosity/).

71. Engel, S. 2013. "The Case for Curiosity." *Educational Leadership* 70: 36–40.

72. Kidd, C., and B. Y. Hayden. 2015. "The Psychology and Neuroscience of Curiosity." *Neuron Perspective* (http://www.celestekidd.com/papers/KiddHayden2015.pdf).

73. Stapp, *Quantum Theory and Free Will*.

74. Ibid.

75. Rohr, R., and M. Morrell. 2016. *The Divine Dance: The Trinity and Your Transformation*. New Kensington, PA: Whitaker House, p. 39.

Julie Brown Yau, PhD, is a psychologist with more than thirty years of experience in somatic and spiritual traditions. Her unique approach blends clinical experience, psychology, physical and subtle body energies, and spiritual perspectives in discussing and healing trauma. She is director of education and program development at Compassionate Care ALS, where she incorporates her knowledge of somatic depth psychology, grief counseling, and contemplative practices to work with individuals and families facing catastrophic illness and death. Julie has a private practice in Laguna Beach, CA, working specifically with developmental trauma.

Foreword writer **Lisa Genova, PhD**, graduated valedictorian, summa cum laude from Bates College with a degree in biopsychology, and received her PhD in neuroscience from Harvard University. Genova has captured a special place in contemporary fiction, writing stories that are equally inspired by neuroscience and the human spirit. She is author of the *New York Times* bestselling novels, *Still Alice*, *Left Neglected*, *Love Anthony*, and *Inside the O'Briens*.

MORE BOOKS

ISBN: 978-1626255029 | US $16.95

ISBN: 978-1684032587 | US $16.95

ISBN: 978-1684031047 | US $16.95

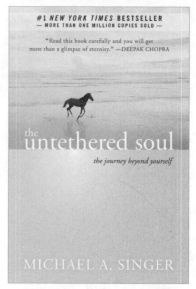

ISBN: 978-1572245372 | US $17.95

newharbingerpublications

NON-DUALITY PRESS | REVEAL PRESS

Sign up *for* our spirituality e-newsletter:

newharbinger.com/join-us